THE ULTIMATE DOLLS' HOUSE BOOK

THE ULTIMATE
DOLLS' HOUSE BOOK

Faith Eaton

Foreword by
Flora Gill Jacobs

Photography by
Matthew Ward

Reader's Digest

The Reader's Digest Association (Canada) Ltd.
Montreal

A DORLING KINDERSLEY BOOK

Project Editor Irene Lyford
Art Editor Kevin Ryan
Editor Lucinda Hawksley
Computer page make-up Mark Bracey
Production Eunice Paterson, Meryl Silbert
Managing Editor Mary-Clare Jerram
Managing Art Editors Spencer Holbrook, Amanda Lunn

Published in Canada in 1994 by
The Reader's Digest Association (Canada) Ltd.
215 Redfern Avenue, Montreal, Quebec H3Z 2V9

First published in Great Britain in 1994
by Dorling Kindersley Limited,
9 Henrietta Street, London WC2E 8PS

CANADIAN CATALOGUING IN PUBLICATION DATA
Eaton, Faith
The ultimate doll's house book

1st Canadian ed.
Includes index
ISBN 0-88850-234-6

1. Dollhouses–History. I. Reader's Digest
Association (Canada). II. Title

NK4893.E38 1994   688.7'23   C94-900277-1

READER'S DIGEST and the Pegasus logo are registered trademarks
of The Reader's Digest Association, Inc.

Text film output by The Right Type, Great Britain
Reproduction by Colourscan, Singapore
Printed and bound in Italy by New Interlitho

94 95 96 97 98 / 5 4 3 2 1

CONTENTS

FOREWORD

Flora Gill Jacobs

IN A DOLLS' HOUSE, "time stands still and a period is preserved as it never can be in a full-sized house. All sorts of things, however ephemeral, are left in a dolls' house that would never remain in a human's."

These are words of mine in the 1965 edition of *A History of Dolls' Houses*. They are repeated here, not only because they help to explain the role of an antique dolls' house as a historical document, but because they relate to a coincidence. "There can be no better example," I continued, "than a nearly modern dolls' house played with in the grim, dark London days of World War II by Miss Faith Eaton, a gifted English doll maker and collector." The author of this beautiful book had once written to me to describe her 1940 dolls' house with its "air raid shelter ... brown sticky paper crosses on its windows, and blackout curtains." Faith Eaton crossed the pages of my book and now, briefly, I cross the pages of hers. I have always maintained that the dolls' house world is small in all respects, and here is yet another example.

PLAYTIME *(ABOVE) To countless small girls in the past, their dolls' houses were well-loved playthings that gave no hint of the role they were to assume, generations later, as reflections of domestic history.*

Small it may be, but this miniature world has expanded greatly in recent years. There has been a renaissance, in which collectors have been collecting old dolls' houses, furnishing new ones, organizing "miniature" clubs, and arranging fairs where dolls' houses and their contents are sold. Books about dolls' houses also have proliferated.

— BIRTH OF A COLLECTOR —

When, in 1945, I embarked upon a history of dolls' houses, and then started to collect (a reversal of the usual procedure), there had never been a "history." At the turn of the century, a learned volume was published in German and Dutch

MEXICAN HOUSE *(BELOW) Found in 1977, covered with dust, in an antique shop in Puebla, Mexico, this mansion is now referred to by the Washington Dolls' House & Toy Museum as its extravaganza. The house is 90in (228cm) high and 72in (183cm) wide, and features a chapel, an aviary, a working elevator, and a roof garden.*

about the magnificent seventeenth- and eighteenth-century Dutch *puppen-huizen*, and there had been books about the elaborate dolls' house presented to Queen Mary by her subjects in 1924. But most antique dealers were slow to notice the charming possibilities that remained in attics till decades later. When I visited London in 1948, several weeks spent prowling in antique shops for old dolls' houses and their furnishings produced only a couple of chairs and a settee.

— GROWING TREND —

In 1975, when the Washington Dolls' House & Toy Museum opened to the public, there were collections or isolated examples in public museums in Britain, Europe, and the United States, and there was Vivien Greene's private museum in Oxford. Small doll museums, with antique dolls on shelves and an odd house nearby, were not unusual. In recent years, however, dolls' house museums have been opening on both sides of the Atlantic. Dolls' houses have become, with many collectors, not only a preoccupation but an addiction – one that is often associated with a degree of dissatisfaction with today's world.

But there is another lure to the dolls' house, which has always existed – an element that was described by A.C. Benson (co-editor, with Sir Lawrence Weaver, of *The Book of the Queen's Dolls' House*) in words that have never yet been surpassed: "There is great beauty in smallness. One gets all the charm of design and color and effect, because you can see so much more in combination and juxaposition..."

In other words, dolls' houses are not only historic, documenting in miniature the architecture, decorative arts, and daily life that they reflect, but they are also seductive. With this volume, illustrated by Matthew Ward's exquisite pictures, which are almost trompe l'oeil in their effect, another wave of dolls' house collectors is almost certain to be seduced.

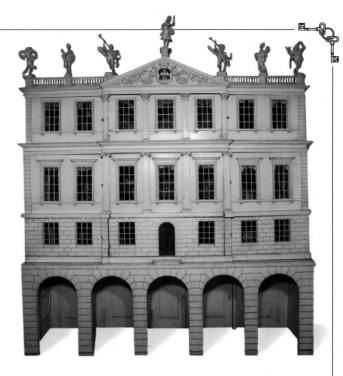

UPPARK *(ABOVE)*
The nine rooms in this English baby house (each opening separately) are all beautifully furnished and are occupied by correctly costumed dolls. The house was taken to Uppark in Sussex in 1747 by Miss Sarah Lethieullier when she married Sir Matthew Fetherstonhaugh.

CHRISTIAN HACKER HOUSE *(BELOW)*
This house, made in Nuremberg c.1900, is typical of those created by Christian Hacker. Although some aspects of designs varied to some extent, other features, such as the lift-off mansard roof and the "French" look illustrated here, were invariably maintained.

INTRODUCTION

Miniatures have an irresistible fascination for both adults and children: adults are intrigued by the skill and artistry involved in the creation of tiny objects, while children are simply entranced. When the doors of a miniature house are opened, revealing comfortably furnished bedrooms, an elegant drawing room, or a kitchen equipped with every utensil imaginable, the magic is complete. We hope that within these pages you too will experience the enchantment.

THERE IS NO AGE LIMIT for dolls' house enthusiasts. For many, their involvement has grown up with them, having first focused on a childhood plaything; some develop their interest by way of related subjects, such as architecture, interior design, or social history; yet others may discover, in their second childhood, a pleasure that they were denied in their first. The fascination of miniature replicas has been experienced since the days of ancient Greece and Rome but, for many dolls' house collectors, the most interesting part of the long history of miniature houses and their furnishings began in the countries of northern Europe, around the middle of the seventeenth century.

— NATIONAL VARIATIONS —

Most dolls' house collectors in the seventeenth and eighteenth centuries lived in Germany, Holland, or in England. The interiors of their miniature houses reflected their own daily lives, illustrating how their homes were furnished. The type of casing chosen to house the collections differed from country to country, however.

German women believed that it was important to teach their young daughters how to be good housewives, so they tended to use miniature houses as educational toys. This is not to say that the children were allowed to treat these small replicas as playthings —

DUTCH CABINET *(LEFT)*
Petronella de la Court's late-seventeenth-century cabinet house reflects the splendor and elegance that epitomized such affluent Dutch collectors' homes. The cabinet itself is a magnificent piece of furniture, and most of the miniature pieces it contains are beautiful objets d'art.

TOO OLD TO PLAY (*ABOVE*)
The two-room dolls' house shown in this detail from an oil painting by Harry Brooker (1848–1941) was obviously a well-loved plaything, which was enjoyed by both boys and girls.

HAMLEYS HOUSE (*RIGHT*)
This house (see pp.96–97) *was a "modern" design when it came from Hamleys toy store as a birthday present in the early 1930s. It is now in honorable retirement in my collection.*

only the room settings that were furnished as kitchens served in this dual capacity – but at least the children were permitted some involvement with what were essentially adults' treasures.

German miniature houses were often elaborately furnished, and were equipped with every household necessity. Although most of them had realistic roofs and side walls, the models usually lacked fronts: the importance of these miniature houses lay with their contents and furnishings, so a facade would have served no particular purpose.

Affluent Dutch men and women were often ardent collectors of porcelain,

paintings, and fine furniture, as well as miniature replicas. As the latter were often very valuable, they were sometimes housed inside a fine cabinet or cupboard that had been designed and adapted to look like the interior of a house.

Dutch cabinet houses, like the German dolls' houses, lacked a realistic, houselike facade; the cabinet doors hid and protected the miniature contents within, and served to emphasize the value of the collectors' possessions. Sara Ploos van Amstel and Petronella de la Court were both particularly enthusiastic Dutch collectors; two of their exquisite cabinet houses are featured in this book (*see pp.24–29; 34–37*).

English collectors in the seventeenth and eighteenth centuries had quite a different attitude.

WAX DOLLS (*LEFT*)
The well-preserved wax dolls in Petronella de la Court's Dutch cabinet house (see pp.24–29) *are all beautifully dressed in late-seventeenth-century costumes.*

For them a baby house was exactly what the description suggested: a small replica of a house with a realistic facade – one that may have been loosely based on, or even deliberately designed to replicate, their own home.

A large number of early dolls' houses and room sets still exist. These are displayed in museums, both national and privately owned, in Europe and North America, and offer a fascinating insight into lifestyles and fashions over the centuries.

— CONTEMPORARY CRAFTSMEN —

Though dolls' house collections nowadays tend to be a combination of adults' and children's "toys," modern examples are usually furnished with at least some pieces made by craftsmen, rather than entirely with mass-produced items. Stimulated by the immense revival of interest in small replica miniatures that has been expressed by collectors, a number of twentieth-century miniaturists are now creating models of such high quality that they equal any that were made in past centuries.

It would appear that the wheel has spun full circle, back to the days when collectors were commissioning craftsmen to make fine miniatures for their cabinets and baby houses. There is one intriguing difference, however. Two hundred years ago, collectors were not merely collecting and displaying miniature

MANWARING HOUSE
(ABOVE) *According to family tradition, this baby house (displayed in Farnham Museum, Hampshire, England) was made by John Manwaring, c.1788, for his four daughters. The interior is unfurnished, but the house has a double staircase and a German-style parapet across both upper stories.*

NUREMBERG KITCHEN
(BELOW) *The Nuremberg kitchen, filled with tiny implements and utensils, was an excellent teaching toy. This fine seventeenth-century example (see pp.56–57) is exhibited in the Washington Dolls' House & Toy Museum, Washington, D.C.*

WALL HANGING (*LEFT*)
A scroll, with a handwritten verse (see below), hangs in the lying-in room of Sara Ploos van Amstel's cabinet house (see pp.34–37).

MODERN ROOM SET
(*RIGHT*) *This room set, fitted with modern American-style furniture, is from a section in my collection that records contemporary ways of life. The occupants work at home, using the latest technology.*

replicas; they were also deliberately recording their own lives and homes. This is illustrated by Sara Ploos van Amstel's insistence that the unusual basement dining room in her Amsterdam home should be reproduced in one of her cabinet houses; it is also inherent in her philosophy, which is expressed in the words on the tiny scroll hanging in the lying-in room in that cabinet house:

> *Everything one sees on earth*
> *Is dolls' stuff, and nothing else.*
> *All that man finds*
> *He plays with like a child.*
> *Ardently he loves for a short while*
> *What he throws away so easily thereafter.*
> *Thus man is, as one finds,*
> *Not only once but always a child.*

Only a few twentieth-century collectors seem to share their ancestors' desire to record their ways of life in miniature; for most, reveling in the past seems preferable to illustrating the present. In the United Kingdom, for example, classic Georgian-style mansions and ornate Victorian town houses are almost always preferred to dolls' houses that depict today's architecture.

— MINIATURE MASTERPIECES —

There is, however, one magnificent example of a twentieth-century miniature house that was designed to display the skills of contemporary British artists and craftsmen and to provide a record of the lifestyle of the British monarchy in the twentieth century. The house was designed by Sir Edwin Lutyens and presented to Queen Mary, wife of Britain's King George V, in 1924.

Although miniature objets d'art, with or without rooms or houses, have long been regarded as suitable gifts for royalty, this is one of the finest ever made. It was an inspired offering, since the queen was passionately interested in furniture, interior decoration, and in collecting miniatures.

Today the house stands behind its glass screens in Windsor Castle, unaltered and immaculate even after 70 years (*see p.16*). But, although it is still called Queen Mary's Dolls' House, the one thing this magnificent miniature building is not, and never should be called, is a dolls' house. Sometimes the distinction between a dolls' house and a miniature house is arguable, but not in this instance; this house is a perfect example of the miniaturist's art, and no doll has ever set foot in it.

MODERN MINIATURES (*BELOW*)
Pieces such as this Chippendale-style chair and the circular rent table, both made by John Hodgson for the Georgian House (see pp.48–51), illustrate the fine work of today's miniaturists.

GRECON DOLLS *(LEFT)*
"Grecon" was the trade name for the wool- and wire-bodied dolls, with cloth heads and metal feet, created by Grete Cohn in the 1940s and 1950s.

When a miniature house or set of rooms has been created in order to display examples of the miniaturist's art, or to illustrate the furniture and decor of a certain period, or to reproduce a particular historic house, the illusion of reality can be marred, and the viewer distracted, by the presence of even the most lifelike doll.

Two dedicated collectors who were both determined to record, in meticulous detail, period styles of architecture and furnishings in their sets of rooms – Mrs. Carlisle in England and Mrs. Thorne in the United States – both chose to leave their rooms unoccupied. It is

interesting that the women were assembling their rooms, quite independently, from the 1920s to the 1950s, and never met or corresponded.

The sumptuously furnished and decorated rooms of the early Dutch, German, and English cabinets and baby houses, on the other hand, were usually inhabited by elaborately and authentically costumed dolls. These delicate wax figures generally enhanced their surroundings by adding a "human" dimension.

John Hodgson, a leading British miniaturist, chose modeled figurines with meticulously painted features for his miniature buildings at Hever Castle *(see pp.48–51)* as he believes these convey a greater impression of movement and realism than conventional dolls' house dolls.

— VALUABLE SURVIVORS —

Of course, "real" (that is, children's) dolls' houses do need occupants, and collectors today pay huge amounts for miniature dolls' house dolls that their original owners purchased with pocket money. Little pegged wooden dolls (which could be bought four for a penny in the 1890s), may sell for up to $225 each (dressed) or $90–$120 (undressed) at auction today. It is amazing that so many of these fragile little playthings have survived; even if they have lost the odd limb or feature, and probably all their clothes, they still retain their ability to charm.

And so do their houses. Whether battered playthings or immaculate models, such is their appeal that most people instantly relate to them; perhaps not always with the delight collectors would deem appropriate, but few, surely, can remain unmoved by the sight of a teapot not much bigger than a tea leaf, or a Georgian mansion balanced on a card table.

JAPANESE MODEL *(ABOVE)* Models such as this were designed as ornaments, for display purposes only. It is not a true dolls' house, but a replica of a traditional-style Japanese house.

JAPANESE CLASS *(RIGHT)* These Japanese doll pupils and their teacher, complete with their original bamboo chairs and tiny blackboard, were exported in the 1890s. (They never had a classroom.)

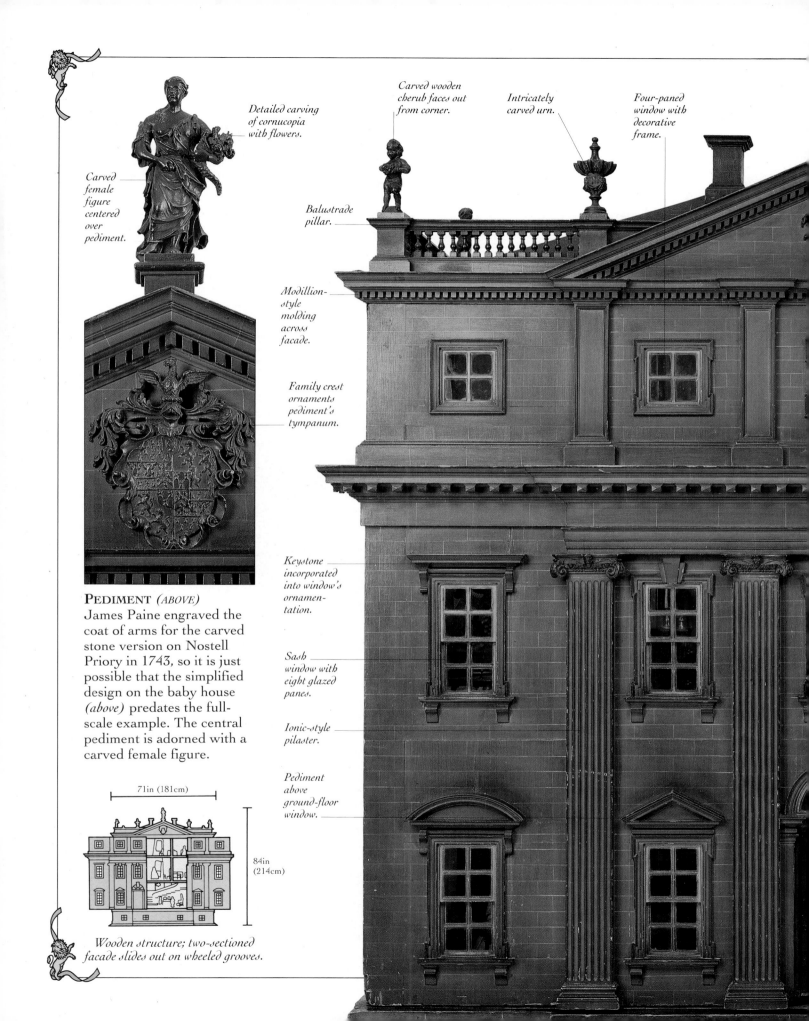

Detailed carving of cornucopia with flowers.

Carved wooden cherub faces out from corner.

Intricately carved urn.

Four-paned window with decorative frame.

Carved female figure centered over pediment.

Balustrade pillar.

Modillion-style molding across facade.

Family crest ornaments pediment's tympanum.

Keystone incorporated into window's ornamentation.

Sash window with eight glazed panes.

Ionic-style pilaster.

Pediment above ground-floor window.

PEDIMENT (ABOVE)

James Paine engraved the coat of arms for the carved stone version on Nostell Priory in 1743, so it is just possible that the simplified design on the baby house (above) predates the full-scale example. The central pediment is adorned with a carved female figure.

71in (181cm)

84in (214cm)

Wooden structure; two-sectioned facade slides out on wheeled grooves.

FINE FURNITURE

DESPITE ITS AGE, the Nostell Priory baby house, which dates from the first half of the eighteenth century, still contains virtually all of its original fixtures, furniture, dolls (dressed in authentic period costumes), and accessories, including the fabrics draping beds and windows, and the wall coverings. The quality of the paintings, porcelain, glass, and silverware is equaled only by that of the furniture, which, according to Winn family tradition, includes pieces by Thomas Chippendale. Certainly many of the designs are his and the workmanship, as exemplified by the pieces on this page, is very fine indeed.

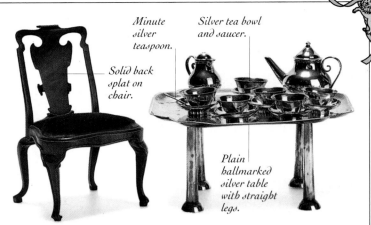

Minute silver teaspoon.

Silver tea bowl and saucer.

Solid back splat on chair.

Plain hallmarked silver table with straight legs.

CHAIR AND TABLE (ABOVE)
The chair is one of many Chippendale-style chairs in the baby house and is from a set of three, plus two sofas. The silver table is less realistic than the tea service, and looks surprisingly modern.

CLOCK (BELOW)
The skill of miniature clockmakers often rivaled that of the craftsmen who produced full-scale time-pieces, as illustrated by this long-case example in a polished walnut case with gilded finials. The silvered dial is marked "Jn. Halifax, Barnsley."

CARD TABLE (BELOW)
The hinged frame of this velvet-covered card table, with oval counter wells in each corner, allows the legs to tuck in under the folded top when not in use. The chair, although relatively crude, has a comfortable, red padded seat.

Blue and white porcelain vase.

Decoratively painted porcelain container.

Bristol blue glass set of decanter and stemmed wineglasses.

Gilded finials surmount clock's hood.

Red velvet-covered top.

Pigeonhole above small pull-out desk drawer.

Oriental-style porcelain jar with lid.

Oval well in each corner, to hold coins or counters.

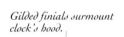

Clockface has gilded decoration, black hands, and silvered dial.

Simple chair with padded seat.

Perfect replica brass handle on drawer.

Polished hall chair.

Chair with turned back spindles.

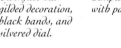

GLAZED WALNUT BUREAU (ABOVE)
Pull-out struts support the hinged desktop of this walnut bureau, which has shelves in the upper glazed cabinet and drawers and pigeonholes below. On top and alongside the bureau are several porcelain pieces.

HALL CHAIRS (LEFT)
In addition to a set of four solid, well-polished hall chairs, there are two spindle-backed models, placed on either side of the marble fireplace.

Long-case clock in fine walnut casing.

CHINESE WALL PANEL

(LEFT) A sumptuous effect is created in the second-floor corner room by the use of vibrant Chinese panels on the walls. Their lively design lifts the atmosphere of an otherwise somber drawing room.

Valance matches bed canopy in next room.

Carved wooden firescreen with floral tapestry panel.

Walnut armchair on cabriole legs.

Walnut stool has upholstered seat.

Ornate valance edged with gold braid.

"Three-tier" fireplace with inset marble hearthstone.

Mirror incorporated into gilt picture frame.

Hallmarked silver dish with lid.

Marble-topped table on wrought-iron brackets.

THIRD FLOOR

The rich, gold-colored curtains and upholstered seating make the boudoir *(left)* an elegant yet comfortable room. A canopied bed dignifies the austere bedroom *(center)*, while a set of charming, carved ivory chairs and a chintz-draped bed with matching curtains distinguish the lying-in room *(right)*.

SECOND FLOOR

Glowing panels enliven the small drawing room *(left)* and, in the bedroom next door, the velvet wall coverings above a wood-paneled dado match the crimson bed hangings. In the drawing room *(right)*, the gilt-edged découpage wall decoration provides a handsome backdrop to the massive splendor of the marble fireplace, which dominates the room.

FIRST FLOOR

The informal dining room *(left)* has a "three-tier" fire-place, with a gilt-framed mirror and painting above the marble fire surround. The hall has a splendid staircase and a set of hall chairs behind a plain table. The kitchen *(right)* seems unnaturally immaculate; the cook, with no food to prepare, has to resort to polishing his equipment.

Nostell Priory Baby House

The Nostell Priory baby house is one of the most magnificent and well-preserved examples of its kind. The fact that it is still housed in the stately home in Yorkshire, England, where it was first created makes it all the more intriguing.

PORTRAITS
(ABOVE)
In 1729, Sir Rowland Winn, the fourth baronet, married Miss Susanna Henshaw, daughter of a lord mayor of London. Lady Winn supervised the interior decoration of the baby house, as well as providing, along with her sister, Miss Henshaw, much of the needlework in the house.

MANY CONJECTURES have been made about the origins of Nostell's famed baby house, including the belief that Thomas Chippendale was involved in its construction, but no concrete evidence exists on this point. It is known that it was begun in 1735, around the same time as work started on Sir Rowland Winn's new house on the grounds of Nostell Priory. The baby house was predominantly an adult "toy," filled with objets d'art and reflecting the lifestyle of its owner, Lady Winn. Although the baby house shares a number of similarities with Nostell Priory, which was redesigned many times and includes modifications by James Paine and Robert Adam, it also bears a resemblance to the Winn's previous home, at Thornton Curtis, Lincolnshire, England (particularly its staircase). Interestingly, the baby house features a balustrade and statues on the roof, ideas that Robert Adam suggested *c.*1780 for Nostell, but which were not put into effect.

THE FACADE
The fine proportions of the Nostell Priory baby house are best appreciated when you can see the whole facade, from the balustraded roof to the false basement section.

SERVANT DOLLS *(ABOVE)*
The dolls of the house are meticulously dressed in mid-eighteenth-century style.

STATELY HOME *(LEFT)*
A print of Nostell Priory from the time when it was the seat of Charles Winn (1795–1874).

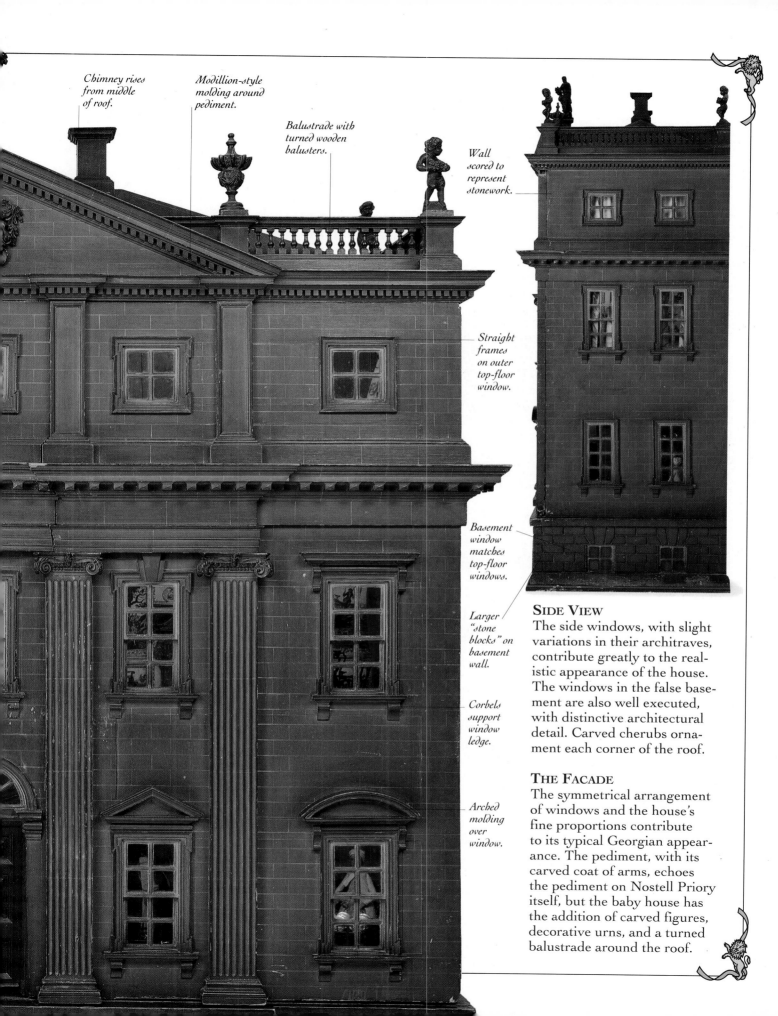

Chimney rises from middle of roof.

Modillion-style molding around pediment.

Balustrade with turned wooden balusters.

Wall scored to represent stonework.

Straight frames on outer top-floor window.

Basement window matches top-floor windows.

Larger "stone blocks" on basement wall.

Corbels support window ledge.

Arched molding over window.

SIDE VIEW

The side windows, with slight variations in their architraves, contribute greatly to the realistic appearance of the house. The windows in the false basement are also well executed, with distinctive architectural detail. Carved cherubs ornament each corner of the roof.

THE FACADE

The symmetrical arrangement of windows and the house's fine proportions contribute to its typical Georgian appearance. The pediment, with its carved coat of arms, echoes the pediment on Nostell Priory itself, but the baby house has the addition of carved figures, decorative urns, and a turned balustrade around the roof.

COLLECTORS' ITEMS

ADULTS IN EIGHTEENTH-CENTURY England and Europe were enthusiastic collectors of small art objects, displaying them in cases or in baby houses. Some English and Dutch metalsmiths specialized in miniatures, advertising themselves as "goldsmiths and toymen." The quality of miniature items in the Nostell Priory baby house – particularly the silver, which includes many solid, hallmarked examples – is very fine indeed.

Unusually thin top rail on chair back.

Plain seat cover edged with band of curtain fabric.

Carved figure decorates fireback.

Carved ivory tongs match grate.

Carved ivory fender matches grate.

Curved top provides ornamental detail.

Simple scalloped edge on valance.

Delicate floral design printed on chintz.

Round bolster covered to match cushion.

Finely quilted silk bed cover.

CARVED IVORY (*ABOVE*)
The ivory grate, with tongs and fender, was probably made to fit the fireplace in the lying-in room. The chair is one of a set of four with cabriole legs and upholstered seats.

WASHSTANDS (*RIGHT*)
The dark wooden stand with triangular drawer holds a silver pitcher and jug. A silver ewer hangs over the bowl on the large silver washstand, and a smaller metal stand holds a painted porcelain set.

KETTLE (*RIGHT*)
This splendid silver kettle, on an elegant silver warming stand, has a decorative, yet practical, turned wooden handle and a wooden knob.

Tiny detailed silver cherub.

Unusually long handle on silver ewer.

Painted flowers decorate bowl.

Tripod base on wooden washstand.

Silver hot-water container with tap.

Lidded silver container.

Silver sifter with perforated lid.

Opening drawer of small table with turned legs.

Three curled legs on kettle stand.

CANOPIED BED (*ABOVE*)
This English lying-in bed is charmingly simple – in contrast with most other examples, which were usually richly ornate in order to impress visitors.

TABLE AND PLATE RACK
(*BELOW*) An impressive collection of silver items is displayed on the table and on the unusual floor-standing plate rack (most racks were wall-hung).

Set of hall-marked silver plates.

Cupboard with painted door panel, diagonally placed over fireplace.

Carved wooden cherub looks out from corner of roof.

Chintz curtains match bed's drapery.

Baby's basket has quilted lining.

Walls decorated with découpaged scenic panels.

Dark red velvet curtains with gold-braid trim.

Chair rail essential to protect wall decorations from damage.

Petit-point tapestry used as carpet.

Rack holds skewers for spit.

Mechanism for turning metal spit.

Lower groove with built-in wheels.

FIREPLACE (*ABOVE*)
The gilded bust, centered on the ornate marble mantelpiece, with its pewter grate and fender, is framed by the gilded carvings around the mantel mirror and on the chimney.

DRAWING ROOM DOOR (*ABOVE*) This elaborately decorated door displays an architrave with modillioned pediment and a carved lintel and door panels, all decorated with gilded molding. The brass door hardware is exquisitely crafted; the handles have a mechanism to open and close the door.

MID-EIGHTEENTH-CENTURY ENGLISH DOLLS

THE NOSTELL PRIORY BABY HOUSE seems caught in a time warp, and its dolls, wearing well-preserved mid-eighteenth-century costumes, make fitting occupants for such a mansion. Much may be learned about the fashions of that period from the dolls' dress: the women and the little girls wear authentic, detailed replicas of the outer garments that were popular at that time, over correctly styled petticoats and shoes. The cream dress with a red pattern is particularly interesting, as the design is finely embroidered in the correct scale for its wearer. Sadly, the only male dolls of the household now remaining are the footman and the cook.

THE LADIES (BELOW)
All of the dolls have well-modeled wax heads and hands and realistic hairstyles. They have been beautifully dressed, with meticulous attention to detail (probably by Lady Winn and her sister). The most elegantly attired (and tallest) doll wears a red silk overdress, over a white silk underskirt, and high-heeled wax boots.

MALE SERVANTS (RIGHT)
Nostell's servant dolls are made of painted wood, in the English tradition. The footman wears Winn livery, and the cook is dressed in immaculate linen.

White wig tied back in pigtail.

Fawn felt coat edged with gold braid.

Round linen cap has red tassel on crown.

Male cook wears apron over vest.

Long linen coat worn over apron.

Long, buttoned yellow waistcoat almost covers knee breeches.

Hole in carved hand to hold ladle.

Carved, painted boot.

Long lace lappets adorn pretty lace-trimmed indoor cap.

Wax doll with small face.

Bonnet-style lawn headgear trimmed with lace and embroidery.

Ribbon-trimmed lace cuffs pinned over sleeves.

"Diamond" brooch on bodice.

Red design embroidered on plain material.

Nurse wears close-fitting lace-trimmed bonnet to match apron.

Double cuff on sleeve of brown dress.

Plain white apron tied in front over pinned collar.

Wax hand molded in lifelike open position.

Full-length printed cotton dress.

Muslin overdress covers blue silk dress.

The
COLLECTION

In this unique collection of miniature houses we offer a broad view of the dolls' house world. Along with adult treasures from the seventeenth and eighteenth centuries and exquisite nineteenth-century models, our selection also includes twentieth-century children's toys and specially commissioned models from museums and private collections around the world.

• HOBBIES HOUSE •

Now a collectors' item, this typical late-1920s English dolls' house was made from plans printed by the magazine Hobbies of Dereham.

COLLECTORS' HOUSES

In past centuries, "collectors' houses" were miniature houses, built to order and filled with fine replicas and art objects made by craftsmen and artists. In this chapter, we feature some magnificent examples of such treasures: two Dutch cabinet houses, and two early German houses, as well as two fine nineteenth-century English and American examples. We include the recently built Georgian House to illustrate the superb work of modern miniaturists.

THE DICTIONARY helpfully defines a collector as "one who collects," but the collector does not find it so easy to state what is meant by the term "dolls' house." Some enthusiasts will use the words to describe only a child's plaything; others, more generously, apply it to any miniature house, whether it is a simple toy for a child or a fine model that has been made for an adult. During the seventeenth and eighteenth centuries, when affluent Dutch, German, and English collectors were commissioning their treasures, the German word for such a structure was *Dockenhaus*, which translates as "miniature house." In England, where the words "toy" and "baby" were employed as adjectives to describe any small artifact, the term for a miniature house at that time was "baby house." Only during the nineteenth century, when simpler versions of miniature houses began to be commercially produced for children to play with and own, did the old words die out and the German word *Puppenhaus*, and its English translation, "dolls' house," become the generally accepted terms to describe all kinds of miniature houses.

— EARLY HOUSES —

Records of miniature houses exist in sixteenth-century German archives. One such account indicates that both Duchess Jacoba (who was born in 1507) and her son, Duke Albrecht of Bavaria, were interested in miniatures: dolls, dolls' houses,

DUTCH CABINET (*LEFT*)
One of Sara Ploos van Amstel's two magnificent cabinet houses, this is displayed at the Gemeentemuseum in The Hague, Holland. It was made in 1743 and is another exquisite example of fine Dutch craftsmanship.

MON PLAISIR *(LEFT)*
The Prince's Porcelain Cabinet is one of the most interesting rooms in Mon Plaisir; experts believe that it is a miniature replica of Princess Augusta Dorothea's own cabinet in her Augustenburg Palace.

DUTCH GARDEN *(ABOVE)*
This enchanting garden, built into the lower central section of Sara Ploos van Amstel's cabinet house (opposite), displays exquisite trompe l'oeil wall paintings, depicting a typically formal Dutch garden layout.

and small-scale models, all of them accurately representing whole towns owned by the duke, featured in their collection. Some of these models now belong to the National Museum in Munich but, unfortunately, the magnificent four-story miniature palace that the duke began in 1557 was destroyed by fire in 1674. Only the inventory remains, giving tantalizing descriptions of the entire building, which included filled wine cellars, stables, and a coach house, as well as accessories in rooms ranging from a ballroom to a bathroom.

— TEACHING AND PLEASURE —

As early as the sixteenth century, some miniature houses were being used as teaching toys. In 1512, for example, the Electress of Saxony gave her three daughters a Christmas present of a dolls' house in which, according to old records, the emphasis was on contents for the kitchen and items for domestic use, rather than on the exquisite objets d'art of the true collectors' house.

Dolls' houses continued to be used as teaching aids throughout the following centuries. Sadly, only a leaflet survives from the replica Nuremberg house commissioned by Frau Anna Köferlin in 1631. In the leaflet, she exhorts, "Look and

learn ... every single piece you see is absolutely necessary in a properly run home."

Other miniature houses, however, were made for pleasure, although they, too, now provide the finest possible aid to our knowledge of social history in past centuries. One superlative example of this is Mon Plaisir, an extravagant project undertaken by Princess Augusta Dorothea von Schwarzburg-Arnstadt, an enthusiastic collector of furniture, paintings, and porcelain. The task engrossed her for over 50 years, taxing the exchequer and patience of her husband, relatives, and church to the limits. It is probable that Mon Plaisir, which was a miniature representation of the princess's court, the town of Arnstadt, and the

CHIMNEY BOY *(RIGHT)*
Every stratum of Arnstadt society is represented in Mon Plaisir: this leather-clad climbing boy, with a realistic wax face, emerges from a kitchen chimney clutching his brush in one hand. The scarf protects his head from soot.

surrounding countryside, was originally displayed in a realistically planned layout. Today the component parts are housed in 80 settings, contained in cases that fill seven galleries in the museum in Arnstadt, Thuringia, Germany.

The display includes more than 400 wax dolls, 10in (25.5cm) in height, all dressed to represent the people living in the palace and in the town: courtiers, merchants, and their households; even nuns and beggars were included.

— HISTORICAL RECORDS —

It is inevitable that any authentic representation of a past way of life will be valuable to later researchers, even if the model was not created for that purpose. Some of the splendid seventeenth- and eighteenth-century German dolls' houses were planned as teaching toys originally, but the cabinet houses owned by Dutch collectors were designed primarily as display cases, which they filled with their collections of miniature treasures, arranged in the realistic settings within. Such houses are just as useful to social historians as designated teaching toys, for their creators were scrupulous about reproducing in miniature their ways of life and contemporary styles of interior decoration. Both of Sara Ploos van Amstel's two fine cabinet houses are invaluable as

QUEEN MARY'S DOLLS' HOUSE *(RIGHT)*
One photograph can barely hint at the magnificence of this spectacular miniature house, which was produced by the best British artists and craftsmen and presented to the queen in 1924. It does, however, offer a glimpse of a few rooms and the "secret garden" in a drawer underneath the building. The house is on display at Windsor Castle, Berkshire, England.

historical records, as she kept detailed note-books, with meticulous accounts of purchases, the prices, and makers.

English baby houses have some advantage over their continental equivalents, for many are still on display in the stately homes to which they were originally brought – mansions whose facades and interiors they often reflect. Nostell Priory, near Wakefield, Yorkshire *(see Introduction, pp.12–13)*, and Uppark, Sussex *(see p.7)*, are such examples.

— WORLDWIDE APPEAL —

Although, in earlier days, the interest in miniature replicas was concentrated largely in Holland, Germany, and in England, there have always been individuals in other parts of the world who have shared the fascination. A curious, two-story, glazed cabinet house in the Musée des Arts Décoratifs, Paris, France, and a single-story Italian baby house in the Museo d'Arte Industriale, Bologna,

ITALIAN BABY HOUSE *(LEFT)*
Within the ornate exterior of this rare c.1700–50 example from the Museo d'Arte Industriale, Bologna, Italy, there is an elaborate interior, which is divided into elegantly gilded, painted, and furnished rooms, all under one frescoed ceiling.

Italy (see p.16), as well as a group of interesting dolls' houses now displayed in museums in Scandinavia, all testify to their universal appeal.

In Asia, the skill of Japanese miniaturists has been displayed for years in charming models. Although dolls' houses are not traditional toys in Japan, many children there have inherited the beautiful miniature replica houses that were made for the annual Dolls' Festivals. Small, intricately carved models of Japanese houses are very collectible, even if not true dolls' houses.

Happily, the miniaturist's skill is still alive and being practiced, to magnificent effect, in the twentieth century, and we have included in this chapter a perfect example of such work. The Georgian House (see pp.48–51) was made and furnished by John Hodgson, with additional pieces by several leading British craftsmen and -women in the miniature field.

— THE PIONEERS —

Nowadays, when it is relatively easy for collectors to find books and museums devoted to dolls' houses, it is hard to believe that less than 40 years ago Flora Gill Jacobs in the United States and Vivien Greene in England were pioneers, the first to record their

knowledge in the books that have guided all subsequent collectors. Their captivating museums – one in Washington, D.C. and one in Oxford, England – have inspired and encouraged other collectors to search for, preserve, and commission the dolls' houses and their contents that now fascinate so many adults all over the world.

VANDERBILT INTERIOR (BELOW)
Although the model has fewer rooms than the real New York mansion, Paul Cumbie followed the basic structure of its interior.

VANDERBILT EXTERIOR (LEFT)
Paul Cumbie created this fine miniature house, based on the c.1883 Vanderbilt mansion at 660 Fifth Avenue in New York.

STROMER HOUSE

— South German; dated 1639 —

T HIS FASCINATING HOUSE, which provides an amazing record of the rooms in an affluent seventeenth-century German home, was presented to the Germanisches National Museum in 1879 by Baron von Stromer – hence the house's popular name (the original owner is not known).

The rooms are cleverly rather than realistically positioned within an open-fronted structure with a central doorway; the sides are painted to represent walls with bottle-glass windows. The internal scale varies, the rooms in the base section being smaller than those on the upper floors – possibly in order to fit in more rooms. Curiously, the casing of the base also differs and, like the roof, was once removable.

Papered wood-grain-effect walls.

Well-filled duvet and mattress increase height of bed.

Fine lawn nightshirt laid out on bed.

Barber's bowl hangs from peg.

Paneling extends only to foot of bed, avoiding stove area.

Balustrade across front of room.

Basket of provisions in storeroom.

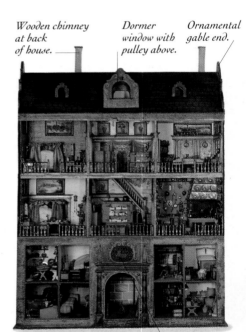

Wooden chimney at back of house.

Dormer window with pulley above.

Ornamental gable end.

THE FACADE

The house has no facade, but the roof features traditionally shaped gables and windows, including a central dormer on which is painted the date 1639.

ENTRANCE DOORS *(BELOW)*

The two arched doors have a trompe l'oeil effect suggesting a vaulted interior.

61½in (156cm)

92½in (235cm)

Open-fronted wooden structure; divided into 15 sections.

Figure of lion set into oval lattice window.

Entrance doors show trompe l'oeil tiled porch floor.

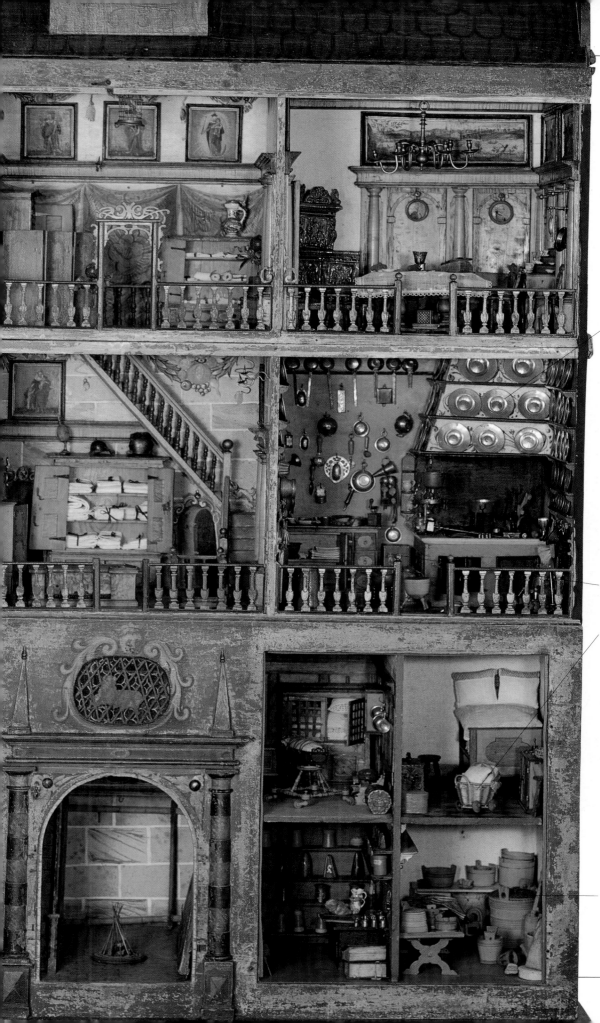

THIRD FLOOR

Both the comfortably furnished bedroom (*left*) and the reception room (*right*) are heated by green ceramic stoves. The ceiling in the hall is painted, as is a decorative frieze. Several fine landscapes and religious paintings hang in the reception room in the area between the paneled walls and the ceiling.

Canopy over hearth useful for warming pewter plates.

SECOND FLOOR

The wood-paneled bedroom (*left*) is heated by a green ceramic stove; next door, on the richly decorated landing, is a well-stocked linen cupboard. In the kitchen (*right*) is an eye-catching collection of metalware, including several shelves of pewter plates around the chimney area and on both side walls.

Decorated meat safe beside hearth.

Baby's bassinet on wheels.

FIRST FLOOR

On each side of the entrance hall, with its painted "cobblestone" floor, stone-effect walls, and poultry cage, is a set of four small rooms, representing stables and a wine cellar (*left*), with a storeroom and servant's bedroom above; and an office/storeroom and laundry (*right*), with two small nurseries above.

Simple but well-equipped laundry.

GERMANISCHES NATIONAL MUSEUM, NUREMBERG

GERMAN AFFLUENCE

THE STROMER HOUSE contains many rare and informative examples of a well-to-do family's possessions in seventeenth-century Germany, as well as spectacular use of wall painting and trompe l'oeil. Such provision makes the lack of occupants regrettable; unused nurseries contain toys and cradles, bedrooms have nightshirts laid out, and no fewer than three linen cupboards store the necessities for the absent household.

CRADLE *(RIGHT)*

A baby could be gently rocked to sleep in this decorative and practical swinging cradle, which is built onto a matching chest with two drawers. It is constructed of plain wood with applied fretwork decoration.

Lace-trimmed lawn coverlet protects cradle's bedding.

Cradle support incorporated into two-drawer chest.

Drawer holds linen for baby and cradle.

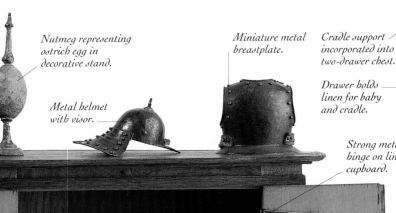

Nutmeg representing ostrich egg in decorative stand.

Metal helmet with visor.

Miniature metal breastplate.

Strong metal hinge on linen cupboard.

Inner surface of door shows back of fretwork panel.

Bundle of clean linen tied with colored ribbon.

Beaded basket for toilet items.

Metal water cistern.

Small metal bell.

Wooden-handled clothes brush.

Brackets originally held water cistern.

Large sponge attached by cord to hook.

Metal wash-basin on curved wooden stand.

Ornamental brush hanging on hook.

Hinged lower cupboard door.

LINEN CUPBOARD *(ABOVE)*

Although German linen cupboards tend to be practical rather than beautiful pieces of furniture, they were often placed in reception rooms or on landings, like this fine natural wood example.

WASHSTAND *(RIGHT)*

A metal water cistern (now stored upside down on top of the washstand) originally hung from brackets above the basin. Two cupboards with paneled doors are built into the washstand.

Metal bed-warmer on stand.

Bold, stylized designs painted on ceiling.

Painted swags of fruit and flowers.

Allegorical oil painting, one of a pair representing "The Virtues."

False bottle-glass window next to bedroom door.

Metal birdcage hangs from ceiling.

Wooden molding matches that in other rooms.

Curved door architrave.

Ornate entrance to top-floor landing.

CEILING SECTION (ABOVE)

The boldly painted ceiling of the top-floor landing, along with the delicate frieze, paintings, and trompe l'oeil curtains on the back wall, give the room a sumptuous air.

Realistic tulips in metal container.

Fragile porcelain tea bowl on matching saucer.

Leather-bound book with paper leaves.

Pewter candle-stick has twisted stem.

Strings attached to pegs.

Open top allows mechanism to be seen.

Keyboard with five black and eight "white" keys.

Metal goblet, of typical German wineglass design.

Bone-handled serving spoon on decorative brass dish.

Delicate metal-bladed knives.

Table legs attached to supporting plinth.

Gold lace trim on tablecloth.

VIRGINAL (ABOVE)

This instrument, a tabletop version of the harpsichord, was popular in the sixteenth and seventeenth centuries, especially with young ladies. This model has eight "white" and five black keys and correctly placed strings and pegs.

TABLE SETTING (LEFT)

Rather surprisingly, this table is from one of the bedrooms. It is set with fine porcelain and bone-handled cutlery on a delicate blue silk tablecloth and is lit by a candle in a turned pewter candlestick with a twisted stem.

UTILITARIAN ITEMS

PERHAPS THE CHIEF GLORY of these fine old German houses lies in the original owners' conviction that the mundane is as worthy of being meticulously recorded in miniature as the exquisite. Indeed, it is usually those everyday items that viewers remember most vividly, as many such houses lack the magnificent collections of objets d'art found in English and Dutch examples. In the Stromer House, the metalwork display in the kitchen is memorable, and items such as the tool chest, with its fine assortment of miniature tools on top, are a joy.

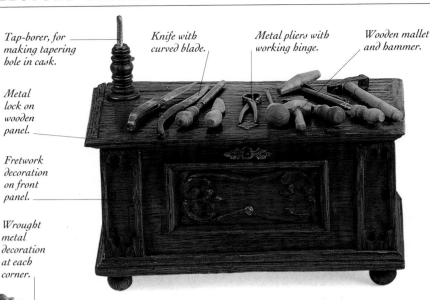

Tap-borer, for making tapering hole in cask.

Knife with curved blade.

Metal pliers with working hinge.

Wooden mallet and hammer.

Metal lock on wooden panel.

Fretwork decoration on front panel.

Wrought metal decoration at each corner.

Metal ornamental clasp incorporated into decoration.

Box decorated with painted floral designs.

Plain wooden box painted red and green.

Decorative metal strip forms leg.

TOOL CHEST (ABOVE)
The importance of practical objects is emphasized by placing this chest in a man-servant's bedroom, rather than in a store- or workroom.

BABY CHAIR (BELOW)
This baby chair, with a fretworked design on the back and sides and a feeding tray across the front, has no legs but is placed directly on the floor.

HATBOX AND CHEST
(ABOVE) Plain wooden boxes, painted chests, and ornamental caskets are found in most of the rooms.

BABY WALKER
(RIGHT) Some baby walkers were tied to a post, so the child could circle, but most were wheeled and untethered, like this miniature model.

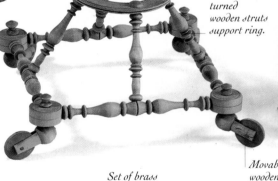

Ornamental turned wooden struts support ring.

Movable wooden wheel.

Carved wooden baby chair, with feeding tray.

TABLE DESK (BELOW)
This is a working table desk of plain black wood, where merchandise was weighed and listed, and deals were celebrated with a drink.

ACCOUNT BOOKS (BELOW)
Heavy leather-bound ledgers such as these provided essential records of business transactions in seventeenth-century households.

Pottery wine pitcher.

Turned wooden candlestick.

Set of brass weights.

Slate in wooden frame.

Sample of fleece.

Wooden stool with three turned legs.

Metal hinge on cupboard door.

Embossed leather cover of account book, dated 1640.

Indexed pages.

Leather-bound journal, dated 1640.

Creel hanging from wall hook.

Pewter plates kept in store-room.

Set of tankards on shelf.

Vegetable basket.

White-painted table with kitchen utensils.

Finely carved and painted horse, one of carriage pair.

Cow in individual stall.

Plain white-washed walls.

Wooden bedstead with fretwork panel on headboard.

Duvet and matching pillow in linen covers.

Towel rail holding linen towel.

Chessboard in green box.

Red and black tile-effect floor.

Wooden tub on table.

Burlap sack, probably full of grain.

Black and white tiled floor.

Set of wooden trugs on floor.

Rack for barrels of beer and wine.

BREAD BASKET *(BELOW)*
Baskets were indispens-able, storing everything from linen to food, as well as being used to transport items about the house.

STOREROOM, BEDROOM, STABLE, AND CELLAR *(ABOVE)* These rooms reflect some practical aspects of maintaining a German town house in 1639: ample storage for stocks of food and drink was essential.

WOODEN COW *(RIGHT)*
Like the two horses in neighboring stalls, the cow has been realistically carved and painted with remarkable attention to anatomical detail.

Willow basket containing homemade breads and rolls.

Cow provides fresh milk for household.

DUTCH CABINET

Petronella de la Court; 1670–90

PETRONELLA DE LA COURT'S magnificent cabinet house is one of the oldest and finest in Holland; the cabinet itself, like other Dutch examples, is a handsome piece of furniture. A few alterations were made in the eighteenth century, and some silver had to be replaced after a theft in the nineteenth century. Otherwise the invaluable 1758 inventories ensure that everything is kept in its original place, giving an amazing insight into daily life in the home of a wealthy late-seventeenth-century merchant.

Petronella de la Court had many collections, of paintings, prints, porcelain, and precious stones, but she is best remembered for this sumptuously furnished cabinet house, commissioned in 1670, which took almost 20 years to complete.

Small entrance hall below entresol office.

81⅛in (207cm)

73in (185cm)

Olivewood cabinet on "barley-sugar" twisted legs.

THE CABINET
The olivewood cabinet is divided into 11 sections on three floors, representing rooms and a garden. The sides of the cabinet are decorated with a pattern of vertical and diagonal veneer strips.

Shelf holds row of lidded wooden jars.

Maid carries basket of game birds.

Slatted wall separates rooms.

Crystal chandelier with nine candles.

Wall covered by large oil painting.

Blue and white Delft-style plate.

Sumptuously
furnished
bedroom.

Brocade
curtains and
upholstery.

Wax doll
wears silk
brocade dress.

Maid attends
to household
laundry.

Maid irons
laundry on
trestle table.

Wooden drying
rack suspended
from ceiling.

CENTRAAL MUSEUM,
UTRECHT

Laundry list
hangs on wall.

THIRD FLOOR
On the left is a
storeroom, with
a second store-
room and maid's
room behind the
slats; next door
is the nursery,
then an elegant
bedroom. On
the far right is
a laundry and
linen room.

SECOND FLOOR
This floor has two
reception rooms,
one on either
side of the low-
ceilinged central
hall, which has
an entresol office
above it. Such a
room is often seen
in seventeenth-
century houses.

FIRST FLOOR
The doors in the
back wall of the
kitchen (left)
lead to a cellar
and a scullery.
The lying-in
room (center)
contains several
ivory pieces,
while the garden
(right) has some
fine ivory figures
and a delicate
ivory pavilion.

WORKS OF ART

DUTCH COLLECTORS in the seventeenth and eighteenth centuries used their cabinet houses as display cases for miniature objets d'art – though the houses also reflected life in their own homes. Possessing both wealth and taste, they created lavishly furnished examples, and their use of the costliest materials, including gold, silver, and ivory, distinguishes these houses from contemporary models in other countries. This magnificent house contains over 1,600 miniature items.

ARMCHAIR (RIGHT)

This brocade-upholstered chair is one of a set in the drawing room. A wooden foot warmer stands in front; heat from the smoldering charcoal escapes through the holes on top.

Arms and legs in "barley-sugar" twisted design.

Tasseled braid around upholstered seat.

Elaborate gilded frame.

Hinged door allows access to inside of foot warmer.

Specially commissioned miniature work.

Biblical figure made of ivory; one of pair.

Carved ivory figure.

Limewood foot warmer holds imitation earthenware charcoal container.

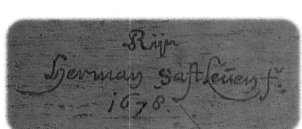

Artist's signature on back of oil painting.

RHINE LANDSCAPE (ABOVE)

Petronella de la Court commissioned both miniature and full-sized paintings from a number of well-known Dutch artists. This landscape, in an ornate gilt frame, is signed on the back by the artist, Herman Saftleven, and dated 1678.

LINEN CUPBOARD (RIGHT)

The Dutch love of "hidden" treasures is not confined to miniature houses concealed within fine cabinets. A splendid trousseau of lace and linen is stored in this elaborate linen cupboard, with carved ivory figures in the door niches.

Linen cupboard filled with lace collars and linen.

Carved ivory relief represents Faith.

Ivory relief represents Hope.

"Barley-sugar" twisted legs.

COMPTOIR (BELOW)

Many seventeenth-century Dutch merchants' homes had a room like this, which served as an office. The well-to-do occupant wears an informal gown and slippers, possibly with a view to relaxing in the small room beyond the doorway in the back wall, which is furnished with a daybed.

SKATES, RAT TRAP, AND SPINNING WHEEL (BELOW/RIGHT)

A pair of wooden skates is kept in the storeroom, along with a rat trap and this finely made spinning wheel with ivory decoration.

Large wood and metal rat trap.

Carved ivory spindle.

Wooden spinning wheel.

Pair of wooden skates with string fastenings.

Letter addressed to "Heer Constantius Popperyus of Pouperys in't Poppe Húis."

Doorway to room with daybed.

Shelves for account books.

LONG-CASE CLOCK (BELOW)

The case of this beautiful clock, which has an English movement, is covered with tortoiseshell; it is decorated with gilded metal friezes and finials and has a small glazed inspection panel.

Lock with key in hinged front panel.

Leather outdoor shoes.

Informal brocaded-silk robe.

Comfortable slippers for indoor use.

Leather-bound books illustrated with prints.

BOOKS AND GLOBE

(BELOW) The globe shown is one of a pair, each mounted on an ebony stand, with brass meridian and longitudinal rings. The fine illustrated books are leather-bound, with gold tooling.

Writing desk with inkwell and quill pen.

Well-stocked drinks case, with green glass flasks.

Brass meridian and longitudinal rings.

Finely painted terrestrial features.

Clock perfectly balanced on marble base.

WORK AND PLAY

ALTHOUGH DUTCH CABINET houses are renowned for their exquisite contents, their owners did not ignore the importance of utilitarian domestic items. To a researcher these miniature replicas, which so faithfully record the equipment used in seventeenth- and eighteenth-century kitchens, laundries, workrooms, and even gardens, are as interesting and valuable as the more elaborate pieces that furnish the reception rooms.

FORMAL GARDEN (BELOW)

The garden is symmetrically laid out with a wonderful combination of practicality (fruit trees espaliered along walls and in tubs), pleasure (flowers in beds, pots, and decorative urns), and fine art. The ivory statues are skillfully carved and match the delicate ivory arbor at the back of the garden.

LAUNDRY EQUIPMENT (BELOW)

The laundry is furnished with a linen press filled with folded linen, a wooden tray of freshly laundered items, and a mouse-trap. The two irons are used for different types of work.

Handle turns to tighten screw, applying pressure to linen.

Pressed and aired woolen nightcap.

Clean, folded linen.

Heavy wooden leaf connected to turning screws.

Wooden carrying tray.

Small trestle table.

Thin plates placed between sheets to keep them flat.

Legs braced by two wooden struts.

Small iron, on heating stand, used for delicate fabrics.

Wood and metal multiple mousetrap.

Fruit trees line garden walls.

Exquisitely carved ivory statue representing one of four seasons.

Arbor constructed of delicate ivory rods.

Heavy iron, on stand, used for household linen.

Upper wall of garden section painted to represent sky.

Painted peacock on mural.

Rosebush with minute paper flowers in "terra-cotta" pot.

Small elderwood wheelbarrow provides utilitarian touch.

Seventeenth-century version of skittles carved in ivory.

Beautifully ornamented ivory urn holds fruit tree.

DUTCH WAX DOLLS

THE ENGLISH CONVENTION that wax dolls were used to represent the upper classes in society, leather the middle classes, and wood the lower classes did not apply in Holland. In this house all the dolls have wax arms and heads with well-molded, lifelike faces. Although the limbs are padded and wired, enabling arms to hold different positions, the dolls' bodies are designed to stand, so those that have been placed in chairs look uncomfortably rigid. Since the farmer doll has an identical twin in another house (in Amsterdam's Rijksmuseum), it is likely that some of the dolls were bought, not commissioned.

STAFF (LEFT)
As the servants in the cabinet house wear the regional costume of Vatersland, it is possible that the de la Court family had a connection with that district. The child (one of the family) wears a lace dress.

FAMILY (BELOW)
The dolls in the cabinet house are fashionably dressed in the Parisian styles that were worn in Holland in the 1680s and 90s. Some costumes, and particularly the womens' headdresses, are very elaborate, with lace featuring predominantly.

Nursemaid wears regional costume.

Well-molded wax face with vivacious expression.

Costume worn by farmers in Vatersland region of Holland.

Leash used to guide young child's steps.

Small child dressed as miniature adult.

Wide baggy trousers.

Elaborate fontange adorns lady's head.

Wax doll's face may be "portrait" head, resembling a real person.

Full-bottomed wig worn by musician.

Red velvet coat, richly trimmed with gold buttons and braid.

Miniature replica violin.

Lace lappets arranged to frame wearer's face.

Beautiful lace jabot.

Apron trimmed with homemade lace.

Music stand with "barley-sugar" twisted support.

Ornate 1680s–90s costume.

CUPBOARD HOUSE

— German; second half of seventeenth century —

ALTHOUGH HOLLAND is the country most noted for its cabinet houses, there are some interesting early German examples. The German rooms, however, were usually housed in cupboards, the difference between cabinet and cupboard houses being not so much in their contents as in the structures that contain the rooms: cabinets are generally fine, decorative pieces of furniture, while cupboards are usually simple, functional containers. But the outward appearance of this German example – a plain, one-shelved cupboard with a paneled drawer in the base – belies the fine quality and exquisite detail of the furnishings and contents contained in the two rooms, arranged as a kitchen and as a sitting room with a bed.

Carved decorative edge on wooden panel.

Molded figure on green-glazed tile.

Metal semi-circular basin on washstand.

Plain varnished wooden cupboard.

Set of pewter plates on shelf.

Row of small, turned pewter mugs.

Large serving dish.

Shelves fill whole kitchen wall.

Hinged lid on pewter tankard.

Turned wooden leg on stand holding stove.

THE FACADE
Apart from some molding around the top, and a paneled drawer front, this simple cupboard, divided into two rooms, is unadorned.

Low painted bench holds utilitarian items.

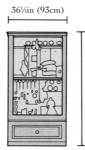

36½in (93cm)

68in (173cm)

Varnished wooden cupboard with one shelf; drawer in base.

PEWTER DISPLAY *(ABOVE)*
The exceptional quality of this beautifully kept, eye-catching display of tableware and kitchen utensils testifies to the renowned skill of Nuremberg's metalworkers.

UPPER ROOM

With the exception of the area just around the stove, the walls are paneled in natural wood with a decorative fretwork finish. The room is fully furnished with a sideboard, table, washstand, chest of drawers, and a bed in the corner, piled high with feather quilts. A six-branched brass candelabrum hangs from the ceiling.

Decorated dishes of blue and white Nuremberg faience on shelf.

Textured paper pasted on wall behind stove.

Wire and wood birdcage with feathered occupant.

Metal candle snuffers hanging from hook.

Wooden stand for ceramic stove.

Plates stored and warmed on hood above hearth.

Skewers hooked onto spit.

Doll wears regional costume.

CERAMIC STOVE *(ABOVE)*

Many continental dolls' houses contain stoves, but few are of such fine quality as this ornate example, covered in intricately molded, green-glazed Nuremberg tiles. The stove is raised on a wooden stand, on a red and white tiled plinth.

LOWER ROOM

With its exceptional display of pewter, wooden items, and kitchen equipment, this is one of the finest known early kitchens. The mechanical spit (dated 1550), the hallmarked, long-handled pans hanging on the back wall, and the wide range of cooking implements and utensils are not just individually valuable; as a detailed reference for the social historian, they are priceless. The cook, with hair tied in two long braids, has unfortunately suffered serious damage to her wax face.

GERMANISCHES NATIONAL MUSEUM, NUREMBERG

FINE CRAFTSMANSHIP

ALL THE SMALLER accessories and household items are particularly well made: some of the spinning implements, for instance, are delicate miniature replicas. The larger pieces of furniture lack their fine finish, however; instead of veneer and carving, these pieces have varnish and fretwork decoration, and the favored wood is pine. As this house, like the Stromer House *(see pp.18–23)*, is intended to reflect the home of a wealthy seventeenth-century German merchant, rather than the interior of a mansion, the rooms and furnishings are entirely appropriate.

Ornamental fretwork on back of dresser.

One of pair of brass candlesticks.

Tiny pair of kid gloves on velvet-topped box.

Out-of-scale metal thimble.

Book hanging by long thread looped around hook.

Metal door handle and lock.

Molding on base of cupboard matches that on bed.

Brass double eagle.

CUPBOARD *(RIGHT)*
The decorative fretwork feature on the cupboard is similar to that on the bed and on the wooden paneling of the sitting-room walls.

Small head pillow with matching down-filled bolster.

Decorative high wooden headboard.

CHANDELIER *(ABOVE)*
Heavy miniature brass chandeliers, with varying numbers of branches for candles, are found in many dolls' houses. Few, though, would have had the double-headed Imperial Eagle for a decoration, as seen on this splendid German example.

WOODEN BED *(RIGHT)*
Looking at the towering mass of bedding on many continental beds, it may seem an impossible feat for anyone to climb on top of or burrow underneath such a mountainous pile – but once in bed, a body's weight made it sink slightly into true featherbedded comfort.

Linen sheet with decorative tassels.

Top feather-filled duvet in white linen cover.

Middle duvet in blue and white checked cover.

Lowest duvet acts as soft mattress.

Straw-filled mattress laid on bed base.

Metal bed-warmer.

Tiny pair of kid slippers with laces.

MECHANICAL SPIT (RIGHT)

This is one of the more sophisticated examples from a variety of spits found in seventeenth-century dolls' house kitchens. Its cog-wheel mechanism turns the skewer holding the meat near the fire on the hearth.

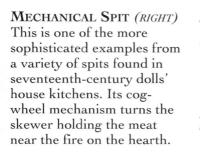

Metal spit with turning mechanism.

Holder for metal skewers.

Skewer in place on spit.

Broad tripod base to balance heavy spit.

Selection of skewers in different sizes.

PEWTERWARE (BELOW)

The kitchen contains a wealth of pewter items, including this lidded pail with an embossed back-section, a teapot, and a kitchen syringe.

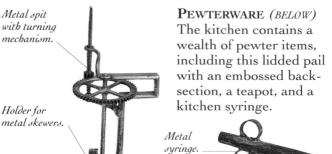

Decorative back on pewter pail.

Pewter teapot with bound handle.

Metal syringe.

SPINDLE AND LACE MAKER

(LEFT) Spinning, weaving, and lace making were important activities in many seventeenth-century households, and this is reflected in the detail on these beautifully made miniature replicas of some of the associated tools and equipment.

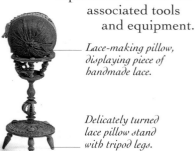

Fleece impaled on holder, ready for spinning.

Highly decorative stand with arms to hold wooden spindles.

Lace-making pillow, displaying piece of handmade lace.

Delicately turned lace pillow stand with tripod legs.

CHOPPING BLOCK AND PLATE CARRIER *(BELOW)*

Kitchen implements in affluent seventeenth-century homes, usually made of wood, were often decorative.

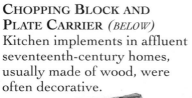

Wooden plate carrier with turned spindle supports.

Butcher's ax with wooden handle and metal blade.

Wooden chopping block with three turned legs.

Maple-wood plates for everyday use.

WAX-FACED DOLL

LIKE THE OTHER TWO occupants of the house, this doll has a stuffed fabric body with wax face and hands, a wig, and beautifully made clothes. He wears a black full-skirted coat with gathered lace jabot and lace-edged shirt cuffs – all in remarkable condition given their age.

Black felt south German hat.

Wide, gathered lace jabot.

Broad black velvet cuffs.

Wax surface of face shows signs of age.

Black full-skirted coat with braid down front.

Pair of kid shoes with tongues and ties.

Lace edging on shirt cuff.

CABINET HOUSE
— Sara Ploos van Amstel; c.1730–50 —

S ARA ROTHE married her neighbor Jacob Ploos van Amstel, a wealthy and cultured merchant, in 1721, but there is no record of any children. They had two homes – a large house in Amsterdam and another in Haarlem. As a rich woman, Sara was able to spend time and money on her collection, and she meticulously recorded contemporary lifestyles in her two magnificent cabinet houses. One, which was designed to fit into a superb walnut cabinet, is now in the Gemeentemuseum in The Hague; the example shown here (sometimes referred to as the Blaauw House) is currently undergoing restoration in the Frans Halsmuseum in Haarlem.

Ornate gilded mirror in nursery.

Curtained "cupboard bed" in paneled wall.

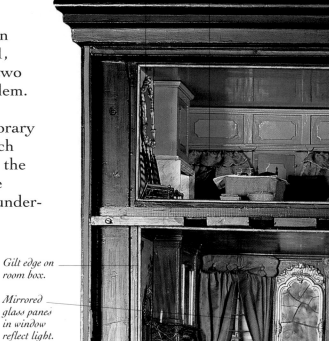

THE FACADE
The realistic facade of this house, with its 14 glazed windows, was revealed only when the solid doors of the magnificent, painted wooden cabinet were opened.

Monogram of van Amstel family above door.

Gilt edge on room box.

Mirrored glass panes in window reflect light.

Mantelpiece painted to resemble marble.

Original painted oak outer door with painted panel.

Panel represents Apollo and the nine Muses.

Side panel decorated to complement doors.

One of room's many portraits of English monarchs.

Splendid display of silver.

Silver coffee-pot made by Cornelis Coutrier.

OUTER DOORS *(ABOVE)*
The outer doors of the cabinet have painted panels representing characters from Greek mythology.

Ratchet mechanism with handle.

SIDE VIEW
The side view shows a painted upper panel, the separation of the basement section from the rooms above, and the mechanism for raising the house to different viewing heights.

Separate part of cabinet contains basement rooms.

Basement kitchen is simply furnished.

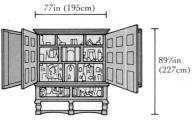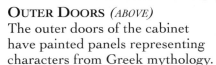

77in (195cm)

89½in (227cm)

Wooden cabinet on mechanized base; two sets of double doors.

Linen press full of laundered sheets.

Japanese screen printed in Augsburg.

Pavilionlike bed with green canopy.

Chest with shelves full of heavy books.

FRANS HALSMUSEUM, HAARLEM

THIRD FLOOR
On this floor are a nursery *(left)* with turquoise-colored paneled walls; a linen room *(center)* with a drying area behind; and a bed-room (originally a storeroom) *(right)*, where a gun rack hangs on the wall.

Oriental porcelain, in Dutch style, arranged on top of linen cupboard.

SECOND FLOOR
A richly furnished music room is on the left, while a painted paneled antechamber *(center)* leads into a reception room with gilded statues. A nurse attends the mother in the lying-in room *(right)*.

FIRST FLOOR
The lantern-lit vestibule separates the magnificent reception room *(left)* (where some of the house's fine silver collection is displayed) from the study *(right)*, which contains medical items and books.

Glazed wall cupboard contains fragile miniature objets d'art.

BASEMENT
A well-stocked kitchen *(left)* shares the basement section with the dining room *(right)*.

MINIATURE REALISM

SARA PLOOS VAN AMSTEL kept meticulous inventories, recording the dates, makers, and often the cost of her purchases. With 250 items in the kitchen alone, and fine examples of miniature objets d'art in every room, her cabinet house is a collector's dream. Particularly noteworthy is the collection of miniature Dutch silver, much of it commissioned from well-known silversmiths such as Arnoldus van Geffen and Jan Borduur.

CLAVICHORD (RIGHT)

This is a replica of an instrument popular in the eighteenth century when music played an important part in home entertainment; family members were often talented amateur musicians.

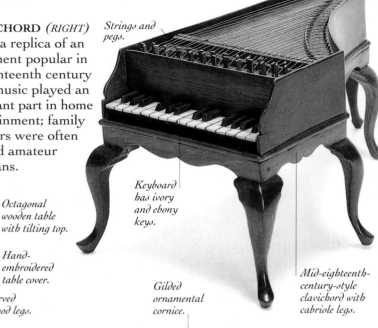

Strings and pegs.

Keyboard has ivory and ebony keys.

Gilded ornamental cornice.

Mid-eighteenth-century-style clavichord with cabriole legs.

CARD TABLE (RIGHT)

The flower design on the cover of this card table was embroidered by Sara in silks on satin. The cover is edged with braid to fit neatly over the table's octagonal edges.

Octagonal wooden table with tilting top.

Hand-embroidered table cover.

Carved tripod legs.

LINEN CUPBOARD (BELOW)

This fine linen cupboard resembles the full-scale cabinet containing Sara Ploos van Amsel's first miniature house, which is now in a museum in The Hague.

Miniature porcelain vase.

PAINTED PANEL (RIGHT)

The delicate gold and red decorations on the moldings of this panel are not original; they were painted in the nineteenth century.

Naturalistic flower painting, possibly by Jurriaan Buttner.

Each section holds a different set of linen.

Walnut-veneered, serpentine-front linen cupboard.

Ornate metal door handle.

Stylized panel, painted in nineteenth century.

Drawer filled with linen and lace.

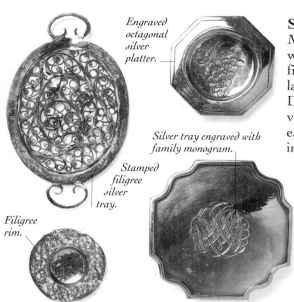

Engraved octagonal silver platter.

SILVERWARE *(LEFT)*
Much of the fine silver-ware, including the two filigree pieces here, is late-seventeenth-century Dutch, but Sara Ploos van Amstel also had earlier examples in her impressive collection.

Copper corner decoration.

Carrying handle set into top panel.

Small drawer holds minute shell collection.

Silver tray engraved with family monogram.

Stamped filigree silver tray.

Filigree rim.

COLLECTOR'S CABINET
(RIGHT) This intriguing late-seventeenth-century ebony-veneered cabinet, with working lock and metal decoration, contains a miniature collection of coral and tiny shells.

Key in working metal lock.

Perfectly balanced legs and stretchers.

MID-EIGHTEENTH-CENTURY WAX DOLLS

THE DIMINUTIVE GIRL DOLL, with her high *fontange*, the nurse, and the reclining male doll have realistic-ally molded and painted wax heads; the dolls' costumes are typical of those worn in the mid-eighteenth century by the characters they represent. According to fascinating notebooks that were kept by Sara Ploos van Amstel, she and her cousin, Nicht Hoogehuyse, dressed a few of the dolls in the house. Most, however, were bought and then redressed especially for Sara by a Frenchman named Jac Castang. The nurse's bonnet, daintily patterned apron, and dress are plainer, cheaper, and more old-fashioned versions of a lady's costume. The householder prefers comfort to fashion, judging by his warm brocaded house-gown, knitted woolen cap and stockings, and heavy shoes.

Wax-headed doll nurse/midwife.

Lace-edged lawn bonnet, tied to frame face.

Knitted cap worn when heavy wig is discarded.

Headdress with high fontange, fashionable in late eighteenth century.

Doll wears cravat and matching cuffs.

Bodice has printed pattern and red lacing.

Crocheted belt with fringed end.

White knitting on pair of tiny needles.

White lace apron.

Plain skirt worn over several petticoats.

VICTORIAN CUPBOARD

—— English; c.1860s with later additions ——

T O OPEN A BEAUTIFUL piece of furniture and find a tiny world encapsulated within is a unique experience. From the seventeenth century onward, cupboards were adapted to display miniature treasures and to record the lifestyles of contemporary households. The Dutch are particularly renowned for creating some of the most exquisite cupboard houses – for example, Sara Ploos van Amstel's conversion of a beautiful cabinet *(see pp. 34–37)*.

Although the British have traditionally preferred baby houses and miniature houses to contain their collections, reflecting architectural style as well as interior decor, there are some fine exceptions. The Victorian house featured here, for example, has been created with great skill within a simple cupboard that gives no indication, from the outside, of the exquisite household within.

Original c.1860s wallpaper.

Set of metal dish covers hangs over dresser.

Oil lamp attached to wall bracket.

Cook's head is china with shiny black painted hair.

Painted metal dachshund.

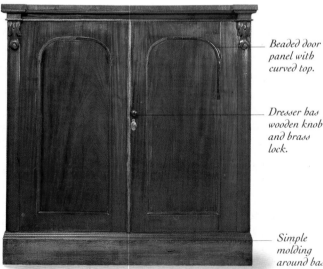

Beaded door panel with curved top.

Dresser has wooden knob and brass lock.

Simple molding around base.

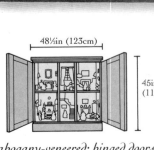

48½in (123cm)

45in (115cm)

Mahogany-veneered; hinged doors; shelved interior.

THE FACADE

The only decoration on this highly polished mahogany-veneered cupboard is the beading around the door panels and the carved corbels on the outer top corners of the doors. The cupboard, which stands on a solid base, has a simple brass lock.

SECOND FLOOR

Doors lead from the central hall, which boasts one of the house's original windows, to the drawing room *(left)* and bedroom *(right)*, both lit by fine metal chandeliers. The windows have trompe l'oeil landscapes behind them. The early Victorian period is vividly evoked in these comfortable rooms by their furnishings, pictures, and ornaments, and also by the well-dressed dolls, which include several wearing original clothing.

Portrait of Queen Victoria's family, by Winterhalter, hangs above mantelpiece.

Metal bed-warmer on floor by half-tester bed.

Carpet in bedroom made from paisley shawl.

Brass picture rail attached to wall.

Hanging central oil lamp lights dining room.

Mantelpiece clock and horses, all made of metal.

FIRST FLOOR

The dining room *(right)* and kitchen *(left)* are separated by an entrance hall, with an elegant quarter-turned staircase lit by a brass and glass lantern. The kitchen is well equipped with copper pots and pans, a dresser filled with china, and an original kitchen stove; the salt box, hanging candle box, and oil lamp on the opposite wall add to the room's charm. The dining room is ready for breakfast, with a laden butler's tray at the side. In the alcove by the fire is a fully stocked bookcase.

VICTORIANA

ALTHOUGH THE FIXTURES and wallpapers in the cupboard house are original, and some of the contents are contemporary, others date from a later period. A few pieces, such as the half-tester bed and the brass picture rails, have been made from old materials by the present owner and her husband. Many of the items, such as the Evans & Cartwright metal washstand, the ornaments, and the furniture (with the exception of the bed), are from the nineteenth century, made over a span of some 50 years.

HALL STAND (BELOW)

On the top shelf of the hall stand, a carved wooden bear holds some letters in its paws, next to a wooden money box shaped like a mailbox. On the center shelf are two straw hats and a hand mirror; a collection of walking sticks is propped in the lower corner.

Half-tester bed has fringed canopy, curtains, and bedspread.

Intricately fretworked bed.

Metal washstand by Evans & Cartwright.

China ewer and basin fit into hole in washstand.

Hall stand made from stained plywood.

China chamberpot usually kept under bed.

Metal hot-water bed-warmer.

Glass walking stick.

TABLE AND CHAIR (BELOW)

Although the table's wooden base is of typical Waltershausen design, the marble top and dolphin ornamentation are unusual. The cast-iron chair is probably a *c.*1840 pincushion, from Gleiwitz in Poland.

BEDROOM PIECES (ABOVE)

These pieces illustrate the range of the house's furnishings. The bed-warmer and washstand are of antique metal, and the china items are typical of those made in the 1890s, while the bed was cleverly constructed in the 1990s from old bookends.

Milk-glass tea set probably made in Thuringia, Germany.

c.1840 cast-iron "Victorian Gothic" chair.

Inset chair seat is padded.

Pedestal table with marble top.

Edwardian metal egg cup holder.

Eggs made of wood.

Silver chafing dish keeps kippers warm.

Coffeepot on stand over alcohol burner.

Folding legs form separate stand for butler's tray.

BUTLER'S TRAY *(LEFT)*
This cherrywood butler's tray was probably made in Waltershausen, *c.*1900. Six eggs in silver egg cups and a dish of kippers promise a delectable breakfast.

"MYNAH BIRD" *(RIGHT)*
The caged "mynah bird" in the kitchen of the cupboard house (an unusual occupant for a dolls' house) was cleverly fashioned from a cake-decoration penguin by the dolls' house owner.

"Mynah bird" occupies cage hanging from kitchen ceiling.

Modern brass replica of Victorian birdcage.

NINETEENTH-CENTURY DOLLS

THE CUPBOARD HOUSE contains 14 mid- to late-nineteenth-century dolls. All but the cook have soft bodies with bisque heads, lower arms, and legs. (Cook is similarly constructed, but her head is of china, with shiny black painted hair.) The fireman and the officer are both in uniform. The "bonnet doll" was carefully dressed in blue and white to match her molded and painted bonnet. The little boy has been reclothed recently in a sailor suit, which was a popular outfit for children in the nineteenth century.

Coiled hose strapped to fireman's back.

Fireman with bisque head and limbs wears original uniform.

Beautiful c.1860s bisque head and shoulders on replica body.

Mustached, bisque-headed officer wears original uniform.

Boy has bisque head and limbs.

Lace-trimmed dress and apron.

Arms are unusually short.

Ax is strapped to fireman's belt.

Heavy thigh boots made of shiny glazed material.

Dachshund made of painted metal.

Sword and decorations are original.

TIFFANY-PLATT

American; made c.1860

W HEN FLORA GILL JACOBS acquired this dolls' house in 1957, it was known as the Tiffany House, in the belief that it had been made for a member of the Tiffany family. Subsequent research revealed that a previous owner bought it at a sale of the Platt family's possessions, and so Mrs. Jacobs renamed it the Tiffany-Platt House.

Behind the imposing facade of this splendid detached New York brownstone are several fine rooms, but, while the two top rooms and those on the ground floor have connecting doors, there are no stairs linking them with the drawing room. Although the location of the dining room on the top floor may seem improbable, it was placed like this when Mrs. Jacobs acquired the house: she decided that the room was too elegant to move to the low-ceilinged "basement."

Framed three-dimensional valentine.

Painted metal wash-stand with toilet set.

Heavy gilded metal display cabinet with porcelain collection.

One of two side windows.

Black-haired china doll holds paper fan.

Ormolu-framed rocking chair with rose-colored upholstery on seat.

Bisque nanny doll in original uniform.

"Frozen Charlotte" china baby doll in rocking cradle.

Red-stained chair with fringed, upholstered seat.

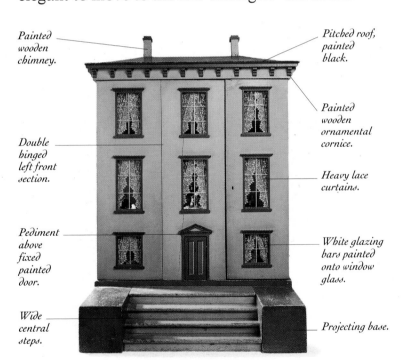

Painted wooden chimney.

Pitched roof, painted black.

Painted wooden ornamental cornice.

Double hinged left front section.

Heavy lace curtains.

Pediment above fixed painted door.

White glazing bars painted onto window glass.

Wide central steps.

Projecting base.

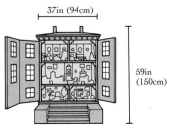

37in (94cm)

59in (150cm)

Painted wooden structure; hinged three-section facade; raised base.

THE FACADE

The relatively small first-floor windows on this mid-nineteenth-century New York town house give it a rather foreshortened appearance; this is accentuated by the outsize front steps on the projecting base, which may have been designed to provide seating for children.

THIRD FLOOR

The rooms on this floor are arranged as a bedroom *(left)* and, oddly, a dining room *(right)*. The dining room contains wood, marble, and gilded metal pieces. In the bedroom, personal possessions include a hatbox and a gilt sewing box.

Gilded pressed metal electric light sconce.

Dark wood jardiniere with pots of fabric plants.

SECOND FLOOR

The drawing room, which occupies the whole second floor, is especially well lit by seven windows and numerous lights. The many delicate gilt items also help lighten this elegant room, and provide a contrast to the dark wooden furniture.

Student's (or library) lamp on bureau.

Gilded metal "tête-à-tête" chairs with silk seats.

Velvet dog and puppies on felt rug.

FIRST FLOOR

The kitchen *(right)* is fully equipped, with items ranging from a metal mangle to a set of muffin tins. The room next door contains a set of red-stained wooden furniture as well as several gilded metal pieces.

WASHINGTON DOLLS'
HOUSE & TOY MUSEUM

MINIATURE OPULENCE

THE ROOMS in the Tiffany-Platt house are filled with fascinating furniture and accessories, including a Waltershausen four-poster bed, still draped with its original curtains, an unusual set of "Chinese teak" furniture, and, in the drawing room, a transitional lamp, which is a perfect period miniature. The kitchen contains my personal favorite – a tiny set of muffin tins.

DISPLAY CABINET (RIGHT)

This fine ormolu cabinet, one of the house's original pieces, is richly decorated with ornate molding above and below the glass panels and on the legs. The cabinet has two gilt-edged shelves displaying some exquisite examples of decorated miniature porcelain.

Milk-glass shade with decorative gilt edge.

PIANO LAMP (LEFT)

This floor lamp – one of many lights in the house – represents a popular design in mid-nineteenth-century drawing rooms. The lamp has an elegant gilded metal stand and a gilt-edged milk-glass shade.

Brass container for kerosene.

Ornamental leaf molding under bowl.

Typical tall stand for piano lamp.

Black flue pipe fits into metal stove.

Brass ornamentation on top of stove.

Gilt-edged shelf holds miniature porcelain.

Ormolu cabinet with back opening.

Elaborately decorated panels and molding.

Solid square base provides stability.

PARLOR STOVE (RIGHT)

The owner of the house followed the fashion current in America at the time, fitting continental-style stoves in front of the fireplaces. This example still has its original flue and ornamental top.

TETE-A-TETE (BELOW)

Sometimes known as a conversation chair or a confidante, this delicate, gilded metal French piece, with two silk-cushioned seats, was the ideal place for gossip.

Padded, red silk-covered chair seats.

Delicate ormolu frame on tête-à-tête chair.

Double seat provides perfect opportunity for private conversation.

Heavily patterned lace curtains and valance.

One of 20 glazed windows on sides and facade of house.

Glazing bars painted on window glass.

Ornamental brass flower studs hold curtains in position.

LACE CURTAINS (ABOVE)

None of the windows in the house have a curtain rod; instead, ornamental flower studs are used to drape the lace at each window. The style cleverly displays the scalloped edge of the heavily patterned lace.

Sand shaker for blotting wet ink.

Photograph album with gilt fret over green cover.

BUREAU *(LEFT)*

The dropfront bureau is a typically fine piece of Waltershausen furniture, made by the Thuringian firm Schneegas, which began manufacturing imitation rosewood furniture in the 1840s.

CHAISE LONGUE *(BELOW)*

The chaise longue, like many of the items in the house, is made of ormolu – a gold-colored metal alloy. Though the decorative seat band is deep, the framework is light-weight and delicate. The seat and the unusual cylindrical cushion are upholstered in crimson damask.

Bolster with gilt lion's head holding decorative ring.

Red damask upholstery.

Chaise longue, part of ormolu furniture set.

PIANO AND MUSIC STAND

(BELOW) This mahogany baby grand piano, made in Boston, Massachusetts, contains a Swiss music box (visible through the glass panel on top) that plays "Three Blind Mice." The gilded metal music stand, holding sheet music for "Exercises," was made in Germany.

Sheet music for "Exercises" rests on music stand.

LAMPS *(LEFT)*

The transitional lamp has a central oil lamp and two branches with electric light bulbs, while the student's lamp has a metal weight on the side opposite the milk-glass shade.

Glass chimney on oil lamp.

Bristol globe.

Milk-glass shade on electric light.

Music box visible through glass panel.

Embossed music stand.

Paper keyboard on mahogany piano.

Delicate ormolu chair is one of drawing room set.

Student's (or library) oil lamp.

Seat cushion upholstered in red silk.

Label indicates music box made in Switzerland.

Ormolu music stand.

ELEGANT RELAXATION

THE TIFFANY-PLATT HOUSE evokes nostalgia for a bygone, preplastic age – a time when dolls' house furniture was made of metal, wood, or cardboard, and dolls were of china, bisque, or composition. It also illustrates the pride taken in creating the stylish, comfortable homes that characterized the late nineteenth century. An added delight is the fact that so many of the pieces in the house are still in their original condition; even if they are sometimes a trifle faded or worn, this merely emphasizes their quality.

FOUR-POSTER BED (RIGHT)
From its draft-excluding top to its carved sides, this Waltershausen bed promises warmth and relaxation; the braided valance and lace-trimmed pink silk curtains and cover enhance the effect. The bed-warmer and chamber pot provide more utilitarian comfort.

METAL BED (BELOW)
The crimson bedspread effectively sets off the gilt tracery on the sides and ends of this late-nineteenth-century metal bed, with its elaborate head and foot panels.

LAMP (LEFT)
This fine miniature version of a popular full-scale table lamp has a pink glass globe around its clear glass chimney.

Decorative finial at each corner.

Wooden top on Waltershausen four-poster bed.

Original lace-trimmed silk curtains.

Lace-over-silk bedspread is original.

Gilt transfer imitates inlay on rosewood.

Metal hot-water bed-warmer.

China chamber pot.

Ornate, gilded metal single bed.

Decorative bed head.

Gilded pierced-metal side panel.

Wooden chair stained dark red.

Crimson bedspread covers deep mattress.

Armrest can be raised or lowered.

Table lamp with gilt base.

SOFA AND CHAIRS (BELOW)
In addition to the sofa and two chairs shown here, the set of nursery furniture includes a dressing table and mirror, all in the same dark red stained wood. The lace-covered cushion on the sofa is trimmed with red ribbon.

Rocking chair upholstered in star-patterned fabric.

Fringed red braid around seat of wooden sofa.

WELL-DRESSED DOLLS

ALL THE DOLLS in the Tiffany-Platt house, which has 11 occupants as well as household pets, wear well-made, distinctive period costumes: the staff's uniforms were commercially made, but the other dolls' clothes may have been handmade. Most of the dolls, including the nanny and the child, have bisque heads and wired soft bodies, but the other three adult dolls on this page have composition heads and hands. Like most American dolls' house dolls, they are "immigrants," imported from Germany and France.

Lace cap matches lace trimming on apron straps.

Nanny wears original uniform.

NANNY AND BABY (LEFT)
Nanny, dressed in a simple brown dress and white lace-trimmed apron, has a bisque head. The tiny unclothed baby doll in the cradle is a Frozen Charlotte, made of glazed china. Both dolls were manufactured in Germany.

Fair-haired, solid china baby doll.

Filigree metal swinging cradle.

DOGS (LEFT)
The bitch and her three puppies are made of wrinkled brown velvet; the white dog is ceramic.

Stand matches filigreed metalwork of cradle.

Bitch and puppies relax on rug, originally a pen wiper.

CHILD AND ADULTS (RIGHT)
The child is a jointed bisque doll, while the adults must be visitors as they, unique among the dolls in the house, have wired, soft bodies with painted composition heads and hands.

Molded top hat.

Bespectacled doll holding pencil.

Painted composition head.

Fashionable bustle on dress.

Molded hat of colored bisque.

Wooden cane.

Rosy-cheeked, jointed bisque doll.

High-heeled, molded bisque boots.

GEORGIAN HOUSE

— English; made by John Hodgson; 1991 —

Blind of colored cardboard behind top-floor window.

THE GEORGIAN HOUSE was the second house that John Hodgson created for the Guthrie Collection at Hever Castle, Edenbridge, Kent, England (the first was a medieval house; the latest is Stuart). Initially conceived as an exhibition of miniature room sets, the collection developed into a uniquely presented display housed in 1:12 scale models, with cutaway sections in the walls revealing specifically chosen rooms.

The Georgian House, based on Palladian-style architecture, is made of painted fiberboard, with fine woods used for the internal doors and furniture. Many features and furnishings were inspired by those at Sledmere House in Yorkshire, England. Several well-known British miniaturists also contributed items to this outstanding example of contemporary craftsmanship.

Open section reveals library, above drawing room, on right side of house.

THE LIBRARY (*ABOVE*)
Details such as the small carpet, embroidered by Patricia Borwick, and the crystal chandelier, by Donald Ward, contribute to this exquisite re-creation of a Georgian interior with its "Chippendale" chairs, partners' desk, and tables of wood and gilt. Three figures are grouped around a flickering fire, created with the aid of fiber optics by Keith Evans, who designed all the lighting in the house.

Dining room table visible through front sash window.

Gravel around base of house.

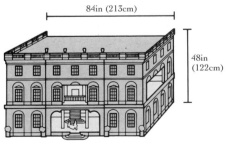

84in (213cm)

48in (122cm)

Painted fiberboard; solid wood doors; nonopening, glazed sash windows; open sections on three sides.

Classical urn on balustrade.

Solid pillar between sections of turned balusters.

Nine-paned sash window.

Head of rainwater pipe initialed "J.H. 1991."

Modillion-style molding under cornice.

THIRD FLOOR
There is no cut-away section on the top floor, but the positions of the sash windows and their blinds have been varied to give it a lived-in appearance.

Pedimented window frame set in recessed arched alcove.

SECOND FLOOR
The beautifully framed cutaway section reveals "marble" columns, gilded filigree balusters, and an imposing portrait of Lady Eglington – a miniature oil painting copied from the original by Reynolds.

Ornamental "stonework" on recessed arch around sash window.

FIRST FLOOR
In the entrance hall, which is furnished with gilded metal pieces, two foot-men struggle to carry a trunk past the marbled columns, up the grand staircase.

Flower-filled "stone" urn on pedestal.

Solid mahogany door to dining room.

Curved flight of steps painted to resemble stone.

Black and white tiled hall floor.

Gilded bronze hall table.

Wall grooved to imitate stonework.

MODERN MINIATURES

THE GEORGIAN HOUSE contains many excellent examples of modern miniaturists' artistry and skill. John Hodgson's beautifully designed and constructed chairs (some of wood, others of gilded cast bronze) are particularly memorable. Also impressive is Karen Griffith's exquisite, handmade 1:12 scale "Wedgwood" bone china dinner service, with a Greek key motif. Each piece bears the monogram "G" for Guthrie.

Fully rigged miniature model of Golden Hind.

Two open and three furled sails.

Authentically replicated painted details.

Tiny "golden hind" on prow.

Gilded bronze candelabrum with five wax candles.

Porcelain bowl by Muriel Hopwood.

Lidded porcelain jar, copied from Ming original.

Delicately patterned table top.

Gilded bronze torchère.

Early Georgian-style table, of gilded bronze.

Mahogany hall table with cabriole legs.

Intricately ornamented tripod base.

Chair with inset seat covered in brocaded silk.

Carved ball and claw foot.

MODEL SHIP *(ABOVE)*

Made by Paul Briggs, this model is a meticulously reproduced replica of the *Golden Hind*, the ship in which Sir Francis Drake became the first English person to circumnavigate the world (1577–80).

TABLE AND CHAIR *(ABOVE)*

John Hodgson designed both the Georgian-style table and the chair, which displays intricate molding, including masks on the "knees." The pieces were cast in bronze, then gilded.

TORCHERE *(ABOVE)*

This imposing gilded bronze torchère, one of a pair in the hall, holds a five-branched candelabrum. It was made by John Hodgson.

Greek key classical motif borders Wedgwood-style porcelain.

Hallmarked silver knife.

Five candles in hallmarked silver candelabrum.

Handblown, eighteenth-century-style glass.

Carved, interwoven, Chippendale-style back splat.

Blown-glass wine bottle with removable cork.

Monogram "G" (for Guthrie) on every dinner-service piece.

One of four hallmarked silver wine coolers.

Finely carved, intricate ribbon pattern on back splat.

Seat cover embroidered in flame-stitch design by Patricia Borwick.

Leather-covered desk top.

Silver inkstand, with two inkwells and quill pen.

Leather-bound book, Country Fayre, published by Lilliput Press in 1986.

Filigree-metal decoration around clock handle.

Tiny etched brass eschutcheon around keyhole.

Back pedestal has cabinet doors instead of drawers.

Battery-operated hands on working clock.

BRACKET CLOCK *(ABOVE)*
Ken Palmer made this fine clock in an ebonized case.

Painted cast-iron dish with molded flower decoration.

DESK AND CHAIR *(ABOVE)*

With four pedestals front and back, containing drawers or cabinets, this is a model of a partners' desk. Alongside is a mahogany Chippendale-style chair with ribbon back and ball and claw feet.

DINING TABLE *(BELOW)*

John Hodgson's mahogany dining table, laden with "Georgian" silver and fine porcelain, is complemented by his set of Chippendale-style chairs. The silverware is by Stuart McCabe, Josie Studd, and Ken Palmer; the glassware by Edward Hall.

MODELED FIGURINE

ALL THE FIGURES – including the servants in the hall, members of the family in the library, and a music master in the drawing room – were made by David Hoyle. Modeled in Milliput (a quick-setting resinous putty) and painted, their costumes reflect eighteenth-century England. John Hodgson chose modeled figurines for the Georgian House as they can be posed in more realistic positions than dolls' house dolls.

White wig, molded as part of head.

Realistic facial expression.

Fichu with modeled folds around shoulders.

Modeled and painted lace-trimmed apron.

Seated figurine represents lady of house.

Mahogany table on four four-legged pedestals.

Modeled quilted underskirt.

SHOPS, SCHOOLS, AND ROOM SETS

Although the basic shape of most shops, schools, and room sets might be described as "just three sides and a base," within these simple confines are found some of the most fascinating scenes imaginable. They have been made for centuries, all over Europe and in the Americas, for a variety of purposes, including religious and secular education. Today, the popularity of such settings among collectors is as wide as their range.

ROOM SETS have a long and ancient history, as discoveries in ancient Greek, Roman, and Egyptian tombs testify. They have been used for a number of different purposes over the years: as playthings, as objets d'art, or as funeral artifacts, chosen to accompany the dead into their next life.

The Greek philosopher Plato once suggested that miniature rooms have an educational function, helping to arouse the interest of boys in building and that of girls in housewifery; Plato's views were often regarded as controversial, however, so it is very unlikely that educational room sets were common in ancient Greece. In Mediterranean countries, room sets seem to have been created almost exclusively for religious purposes, with nativity scenes being the most usual example.

Farther north, in Europe, room sets had a more secular use. In Germany particularly, mothers used them to help teach their young daughters the

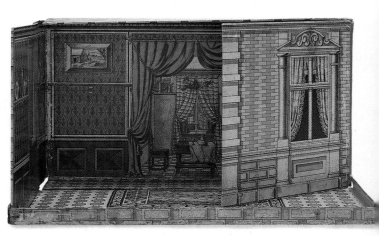

BUTCHER'S SHOP *(LEFT)*
A plaque inscribed "Milligans, Dumfries, 1843" on the facade of this splendid butcher's shop commemorates a real-life family who have been butchers in Scotland since 1820.

FOLDING ROOM *(ABOVE)*
The trompe l'oeil on the back wall of this room is particularly effective and illustrates the high quality of printing on German lithographed room sets in the late nineteenth century.

PERUVIAN SHOP (*RIGHT*)
Exuberantly painted in traditional Peruvian folk-art style, this little wooden shop positively glows. It was made and painted by I. Lopez of Aurocucho, Peru, and contains seven modeled figures and a profusion of fabrics and hats that hang on the walls and spill over the counter.

home management skills required in adult life. Miniature kitchens were especially popular, and a number of examples exist that date from the mid-seventeenth century onward. So-called Nuremberg kitchens became famous throughout Europe, although kitchens were also made in Augsburg, another German toy-making center.

The tiny utensils that were crafted for these kitchens in ceramic, silver, and in other less precious metals, attracted the attention of collectors, who added some particularly fine examples to the collections of decorative miniature reception rooms that were so popular during the nineteenth century.

— MODERN COLLECTIBLES —

Although American and British collectors have traditionally preferred dolls' houses, they have never ignored room settings. Indeed many modern collectors now prefer room sets to dolls' houses because they take up less display space. Two superb examples are the French Parlor exhibited in Flora Gill Jacobs's Washington Dolls' House & Toy Museum *(see pp.60–61)*, and the two-room setting with Rock & Graner furniture from a private collection in England *(see pp.64–65)*. Twentieth-century collectors have added bathrooms to their displays of room sets; painted tin examples with complex plumbing systems are now attracting increasing attention *(see pp.70–71)*. (Modern plastic versions are beginning to become available for popular dolls, such as Barbie, who already have everything else they need.)

A growing trend among both amateur and professional artist-craftsmen is to produce fully equipped miniature workshops; toy and dolls' house makers' studios are predictable favorites. On a similar theme, a friend of mine made the fascinating, 1930s-style Veterinarian's Office *(see p.55)* to commemorate her husband's profession.

Even cheap and cheerful twentieth-century toy rooms, which were originally manufactured as playthings for children, are now extremely collectable. The small, three-walled tinplate rooms that

A & P STORE (*LEFT*)
Part of a 1940s promotion for the early American supermarket, this store provided the basis for a children's game. Posters on the walls also urged its customers to invest in US defense bonds.

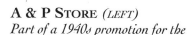

MARX ROOMS (RIGHT)
The 1920s American toy manufacturer Louis Marx produced two series of litho-graphed tin rooms – the Newlywed set, and these examples from the Home Town series, which included stores and other buildings. Each set contained six rooms.

were produced by the American firm Louis Marx, and sold at pocket-money prices by Woolworths and similar stores in the 1920s, now attract the attention of collectors at auction.

— MINIATURE EXTRAVAGANZA —

Three women who indulged their enthusiasm for miniatures beyond most collectors' wildest dreams have each left fascinating and illuminating records for others to admire and study. In 1704 Princess Augusta Dorothea von Schwarzburg-Arnstadt began work on Mon Plaisir, a miniature complex that replicated her court, the town, and the surrounding countryside, peopled with 400 dolls dressed to represent all strata of society. Mon Plaisir bankrupted Princess Augusta Dorothea, who died in 1751, but social historians, costume researchers, and all who appreciate miniature artistry owe her a debt that can never be repaid.

During the 1920s, two other women – Mrs. Narcissa Thorne (née Niblack), an American, and Mrs. Katherine Carlisle (née Apcar) in England – each created a series of rooms recording interior decoration over the centuries. Both commissioned fine craftsmen and artists to furnish their rooms, but there the similarity ends: Mrs. Thorne's rooms, now displayed in the Art Institute of Chicago, were created for educational purposes; Mrs. Carlisle's rooms, which were bequeathed to the English National Trust, were personal records and reflect her lifelong love of fine needlework.

— INTERNATIONAL SHOPPING —

Miniature shops have long been popular: early versions often represented market stands, but by 1800, both shops and stands were common German toys. By the beginning of the twentieth century, every kind of shop was being made in the

SCHOOLROOM (LEFT)
A nun, dressed in her black habit, teaches this class of attentive, neatly uniformed pupils in a Spanish convent school. The room, complete with desks and wall charts, folds up into the box that constitutes the walls.

main toy-producing countries. Each one had its specialities: England was famous for its butchers' shops, and the United States for the use of lithographed wood and paper board. The Milliner's Shop (*see pp.66–67*) is typical of the lavishly decorated shops made in Germany and France.

Printed cardboard shops and stores were popular playthings, as they were both colorful and cheap. Post offices came with stamps and telegrams, drapers' shops with bolts of fabric – and, for less than the cost of one fine wooden example, you could have a whole street of shops.

Several South American countries are now well known for their cheerfully decorated pottery examples and, over the years, China and Japan have produced detailed miniature stands and shops stocked with a wide variety of tiny goods.

— LEARNING IS FUN —

Schoolrooms were also produced – some as teaching toys (one delightful Spanish schoolroom has 26 pupils representing alphabet letters), while others, in elaborately equipped settings, appealed to adults as collector's items. The best-known examples were produced in Europe, their pupils and teachers usually French or German wooden or bisque dolls, provided with books, slates, and maps. There are examples from other parts of the world, however: one schoolroom in my collection is the engaging *c.*1890 Japanese class (*see p.12*), all seated on bamboo chairs and dressed in traditional kimonos. Modern versions of schools

NUREMBERG COOKBOOK (*RIGHT*)
A rare treasure from the Washington Dolls' House & Toy Museum is this tiny book, which was printed in Nuremberg in 1858. The cover illustration shows that miniature kitchens were playthings as well as teaching toys.

are rarely found, but both individual craftsmen and manufacturing companies are still producing shops and room settings made of wood, cardboard, or plastic. There are also many do-it-yourself kits and cut-out books on the market that can be folded into highly satisfactory room settings.

Whether simple and cheap, or created by artists and craftsmen as specially commissioned orders, room sets, in all their variety, have retained their popularity over the centuries, and seem highly likely to go on doing so for many years to come.

VETERINARIAN'S OFFICE (*BELOW*)
This delightfully evocative two-room setting was created by the English owner as a souvenir of her husband's place of work during the 1930s. The contents of the rooms include a tray of tiny medical instruments and several waiting patients.

GERMAN KITCHEN

— *Nuremberg kitchen; made in Germany c.1800* —

TEACHING BY MEANS OF "SHOW AND TELL" sessions has, for centuries, provided a valuable method of imparting information to children. Traditionally, and particularly in Germany, mothers have instructed their daughters in housekeeping skills. This *c.*1800 Nuremberg kitchen was designed specifically as an aid to educating girls for the roles assigned to them in adult life at that time. Room settings, rather than complete houses, have always been favored for educational purposes in Europe, and kitchens were produced in large quantity. Designs for these ranged from a simple boxlike room, with a painted hearth and a few pots and pans, to elaborate settings equipped with carved mantels, glazed cupboards, and shelves weighed down with crockery, pots, and cooking implements – and including, of course, a cook.

THE KITCHEN
Because the toy kitchen is a teaching aid, the contents are considered more important than the structure of the room itself. However, most kitchens are equipped with hearths and mantels, shelves, and wall hooks. This example, which is too early to boast a stove, has an open hearth; its fine chimney is both functional and ornamental.

Side shelf holds pottery jugs and jars.

Pan hangs on wooden peg.

Tin-lined copper pan is one of set.

Finely carved hairstyle.

Well-painted character face.

COOK (*LEFT*)
With her lifelike expression and posture and well-made clothing, this doll originally came from a Christmas crèche – a religious "educational aid" often found in southern Germany.

Extra large hands typical of crèche figures.

Tin scoop for flour or grain.

Cook wears embroidered apron.

Polished pewter table candlestick.

Heavy turned brass caldron.

36in (91cm)

17in (43cm)

Oval tin-lined copper container.

Painted wooden structure of back, sides, and floor.

Paper floor covering with printed pattern.

Barrel-shaped wooden storage jar with lid.

Chafing dish stands on metal tripod with handle.

Wooden-handled iron rests on trivet.

Oil lamp with saucer base.

Pottery vase for carrying sausages in hot water from kitchen to dining room.

Long-handled ax.

Decorative flue on carved wooden mantel.

Pewter plates warming on widest chimney shelf.

IRON, LAMP, AND JUG (ABOVE)
These items, all realistic miniature replicas, are typical of those found in a well-equipped eighteenth-century kitchen. The iron is specifically shaped for pressing sleeves.

CHOPPING BLOCK (RIGHT)
The three-legged wooden block provides Cook with a strong base for chopping wood for the fire or cutting up meat. On the block are an ax and a two-handled cutter with curved blade.

Tin plate cover.

Firewood visible under open hearth.

Hinged copper firescreen with handle.

Metal scales hang from wall peg.

Copper water jar with lid.

SCHOOL EQUIPMENT
(RIGHT) The wooden desks, with opening lids and attached seats, were all in the schoolroom originally, along with the blackboard. The cardboard slates, the school bell, and the exercise books with marbled-paper covers, all German-made, were later additions.

Wooden desk with seat attached.

Exercise book with marbled cover.

Pegs secure blackboard to easel.

Sponge for wiping slate, attached by string.

Illustrated wall map of Yonne region of France.

Painted metal school clock in "brass" case is replacement. Metal face is marked "H.H. Paris."

Wooden walls covered in plain paper.

Little girl wears fashionable buttoned blue boots.

Wood effect around side and back walls.

Paper floor covering with printed diamond pattern.

Front floor extension is slightly lower than main floor level.

Large red satchel contains books.

Smaller desk seats youngest pupil, with elaborate hat.

FRENCH SCHOOLROOM

French, with additional German pieces; c.1880–1900

Jointed bisque doll with glass eyes and mohair wig.

MANY VERSIONS of the ever-popular toy schoolroom were produced in a three-sided box form. Often, if the room had a fourth wall, it was hinged to fold down flat at the front, forming part of the floor. This example, which has pale blue walls and a diamond tile-effect floor paper, is a little unusual as the fourth wall is shaped, suggesting an apron stage, which adds greatly to the charm of the setting. Although the room and its furniture, including the six wooden desks and the blackboard, are French, many of the other contents, such as the pupils' large red satchels and writing slates, with tiny pieces of sponge attached by string, are from Germany.

All the pupils are jointed bisque dolls with glass eyes and mohair wigs. None of them are wearing the traditional French schoolchild's black overall, so their clothes are more easily seen and admired. They are well dressed in a wide variety of outfits, from the pleated red dress and lace apron of the small doll standing at the left of the schoolroom, to the navy blue outfits with sailor collars worn by two dolls on the right. Three types of nineteenth-century children's footwear are displayed: shoes with ankle straps, shoes with two straps, and buttoned boots.

THE SCHOOLROOM

One of the most striking features in the schoolroom, apart from the pupils, is the set of wall maps depicting four French regions: L'Ille-et-Vilaine, Basses Alpes, Yonne, and Drôme. The surrounding sketches of local historical buildings add greatly to the geographical detail.

Blackboard rests on simple wooden easel.

Pupil wears navy blue sailor suit with white collar.

Metal school bell with wooden handle and metal clapper.

WASHINGTON DOLLS'
HOUSE & TOY MUSEUM

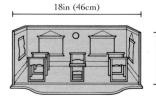

Box-shaped room with three walls and front flap.

FRENCH PARLOR
—— *French manufacturer; c.1880* ——

R OOM SETTINGS, always more popular in Europe than in the United States and Britain, where dolls' houses were preferred, were produced mainly in Germany and France. In their heyday in the nineteenth century, they were designed in various styles, from the simple box shape to elaborately decorated two-room sets with an interconnecting door or archway.

This parlor is a fascinating example of *c.*1880 French elegance and charm; it also shows French ingenuity, for the whole room, when cleared of furniture, folds into a box whose base and front wall double as the "carpeted" floor when open.

The room's sumptuous appearance owes much to the rich, gilt-patterned wallpaper, above a dado of red flocked wallpaper, and the elegant curtains. Although most room sets were sold complete with furniture, the owner could add dolls and various accessories to enhance the appeal, as in this case.

Painted wooden container holds plant with delicate white flowers.

Front wall of box folds down to extend floor space.

TEA SET *(BELOW)*
This enchanting little seven-piece porcelain tea set, from the Sèvres works near Paris, is patterned with tiny roses, and has a matching tray.

THE PARLOR
All the ornaments, the books, and the newspaper, *Petit Journal pour Rire*, are later additions, but the furniture, pictures, and mirrors are original. The furniture includes an oval table, a sideboard, and five chairs upholstered in imitation leather. Both dolls are jointed bisques with glass eyes.

Gilt detail on oval tray.

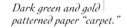

16in (40cm)

8½in (22cm)

Wooden walls fold into box; two angled windows.

Dark green and gold patterned paper "carpet."

Chair, with narrow black paper strip imitating inlay, is one of set of five.

Decorative gold border.

Green wallpaper with gold star pattern above dado of crimson flocked paper.

Lace curtains adorn paper-framed window.

Striped green taffeta curtains with narrow gold braid trim.

Glass window set diagonally across one corner of room.

One of pair of hanging mirrors in gold paper frames.

Fragile fluted glass vase with gilded base.

Patterned wool rug with fringe on all sides, worked in cross-stitch.

Jointed bisque doll holds cup-and-ball toy.

Miniature book dated 1895, Les Rondes de l'Enfance, has illustrated words and music.

WASHINGTON DOLLS' HOUSE & TOY MUSEUM

GENERAL STORE

German; second half of nineteenth century

THIS IS A RARE EXAMPLE of a shop from Waltershausen, a toy-making center in Thuringia, in central Germany. The area is renowned for the imitation rosewood dolls' house furniture made by Schneegas, a firm founded there in the 1840s.

German toy makers are well known for their miniature shops, which have been sold and exported for decades. Shops and stands are still popular in the twentieth century, especially the German *Christkindlemarkt* stands, which are filled with an array of Christmas decorations, food, and toys. Until the mid-eighteenth century, miniature goods were usually depicted as being sold from stands, but by 1800 German toy sellers were offering shops as well: Bestelmeier's 1793 catalogs show examples, and nineteenth-century Nuremberg toy catalogs contain a splendid variety.

"Cigarren" (cigars) stamped on lid of box.

Wooden box still contains some real cigars.

Bottle labeled "Kümmel" (cumin/caraway-flavored liqueur).

Gilt-stenciled griffin supports shop sign.

CIGARS AND KÜMMEL (ABOVE)
Smokers and drinkers are well provided for in this shop: several drawers contain tobacco, and a cask supplements the selection of bottled wine, spirits, and liqueurs.

Gilt stenciling gives effect of inlaid rosewood.

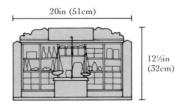

20in (51cm)

12½in (32cm)

Painted wooden structure; open top and front.

Printed paper on floor has unusual pattern and color.

Drawer contains salt ("Salz").

Small metal knob on each drawer.

All drawers carefully stenciled with identical decoration.

Shop sign reads "Materialwaaren" (general store).

Handwritten Italian label on marble jar containing pepper.

THE SHOP INTERIOR

Although this shop is typical in shape and structure of many made commercially in nineteenth-century Germany, its finish makes it unusual. The distinctive Waltershausen stenciled decoration is not often seen on shops, but, as this example illustrates, it is effective and eye-catching when used in this way.

Brass balance attached to plain wooden counter.

Unlabeled, polished wooden cask probably held beer.

Skeins of wool displayed alongside other goods.

Label suggests box of soap was imported from Italy.

TWO-ROOM SETTING

—— German; Rock & Graner furniture; c.1880–1900 ——

WURTTEMBERG, IN SOUTHWEST GERMANY, produced many notable toy makers. Apart from the Schoenhut family *(see pp.92–93)*, one of the best-known names today is Rock & Graner, a firm renowned for the pressed tinplate dolls' house furniture that it started making *c.*1850.

This two-room setting, with its Rock & Graner furniture, was bought in Zurich, Switzerland, at the turn of the century; it is completely furnished with metal items, mostly Rock & Graner's distinctive dark brown pieces, hand painted to resemble woodgrain. These contrast well with the delicate pale wallpapers, light and bright curtains, and warm-toned floors, all of which were part of the original room setting.

THE INTERIOR
The curtains and wall- and floor papers in this setting are original, but many decorative items, including gilt picture frames, mirrors, flower-filled jardinieres, and clocks, have been added.

Rock & Graner settee with silk-covered seat, from drawing room set.

Gilt metal clip holds lace valance in place.

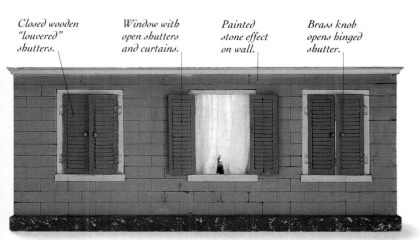

Closed wooden "louvered" shutters.

Window with open shutters and curtains.

Painted stone effect on wall.

Brass knob opens hinged shutter.

THE EXTERIOR

Each of the three glazed windows on the back wall is fitted with a pair of hinged, green-painted "louvered" shutters.

Metal flue runs from stove to wall.

STOVE (RIGHT)

This elegant stove with attached flue provides heating in the bedroom. It is finished in enamel with two gold bands.

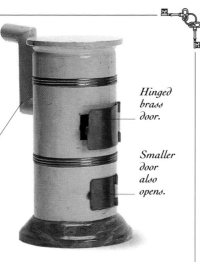

Hinged brass door.

Smaller door also opens.

Rock & Graner jardiniere filled with flowering plants.

Hinged lid of washstand open, revealing toilet items inside.

Decorative valance of lace, braid, and beads.

Metal oil lamp with milk-glass bowl and glass chimney.

SIDEBOARD (BELOW)

The upper shelf of this Rock & Graner sideboard displays a clock and two pictures in gilt frames; the shelf is supported by two gilded sea serpents.

Gilded metal light fixture.

Coiled beeswax candle.

Painted metal plaque is one of a pair.

Metal sideboard painted to resemble woodgrain.

Rock & Graner painted metal bed.

32½in (83cm)

14½in (37cm)

Two-room setting; three glazed windows with hinged shutters.

MILLINER'S SHOP

German; imported by F.A.O. Schwarz of New York; c.1900

THE RICHLY DECORATED interior of the milliner's shop provides a lavish setting for the elegant customers as they make their selection from the models on display. The gilded rococo molding may seem a trifle florid, but the delicate, restrained patterns of the wallpaper and floor covering are entirely suited to such an establishment. Many similarly constructed shops appeared in catalogs around the turn of the century; pillars and wall units were added to the basic boxlike shape to create a variety of styles and shapes, which were then decorated appropriately – be it for a butcher, a merchant, or a stylish dressmaker.

This shop still has its original label, indicating that it came from the famous New York toy store F.A.O. Schwarz, whose catalogs included, for many years, a wide variety of shops, most imported from Germany.

HATS A LA MODE *(BELOW)* With its opulent decor, gilt-framed mirrors, glazed display cases, and many accessories, this was quite an elaborate toy originally. The cash register and the two bisque-headed dolls are later additions.

Original delicately patterned wallpaper.

Glazed door hinged to open.

Miniature spools of thread on holder.

Narrow straw braiding sewn together to form hat.

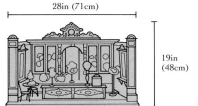

German lettering shows origin.

Price springs up when key is pressed.

CASH REGISTER
(LEFT) Accessories like this intricately embossed small metal cash register, with working keys, add greatly to the shop's charm and authenticity.

Gilded metal chair with round wire-mesh seat, for customers' convenience.

28in (71cm)

19in (48cm)

Painted wooden three-sided shop; open front and top.

Main floor area covered with painted, patterned paper.

Round, three-legged gilded metal table is part of set that includes settee and chairs.

Painted, gilded molding on front of movable counter.

Mirrored walls in alcove reflect millinery.

Clockface of gilded and printed paper.

Ornate gilded molding on ornamental pediment.

HATSTAND (*LEFT*)
The gilded metal branches of the hatstand rise from a central stem on a weighted base; each branch displays a uniquely designed hat.

Wall mirror with gilded molding matches back pediment.

Gilded metal hand mirror for customers' use.

Fashionably dressed milliner doll has molded bisque head.

Delicate gilded metal oil lamp with translucent blown-glass bowl.

Bisque customer doll with well-designed wig supporting elaborate hat.

WASHINGTON DOLLS' HOUSE & TOY MUSEUM

BUTCHER'S SHOP

German; made by Christian Hacker; c.1900

Removable pediment held in place by pins.

THIS BUTCHER'S SHOP, which was given to a young English girl *c.*1905, was made by the German toy maker Christian Hacker, probably around the turn of the century. Based in Nuremberg, the firm began producing dolls' houses and shops in the mid-1870s. Christian Hacker also made dolls' house furniture, another popular line, and toy kitchens Like the shops, these were regarded as educational aids in teaching young girls household management skills – hence the degree of realism in the modeling and painting of the cuts of meat.

As the shop was a plaything as well as a teaching toy, it is surprising that it has remained so well stocked with wares and equipment. The survival of the realistically modeled butcher in his traditional costume is particularly fortunate.

Original wallpaper suggests tiles.

Whole carcass hangs on hook.

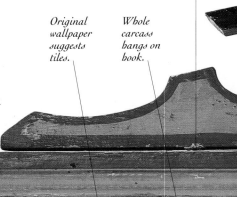

OVERHEAD VIEW
The fixed counter provides a display area for meat as well as a cutting surface; a meat cleaver and selection of knives are visible here, as is the original diamond-patterned floor paper. The cash booth is movable.

Shop has open top behind fascia.

Black outer skin of carcass flocked for greater realism.

Meat hangs from rack in window.

BUTCHER'S MEAT
(RIGHT) All types of meat are sold here, including wild boar. The meat is cut in the continental way, providing a clue to the origins of the shop and its contents.

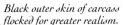

Realistically modeled and painted meat.

16in (41cm)

13in (34cm)

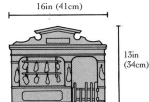

Open box design; hinged gate and cash booth door.

Characteristic Christian Hacker paintwork in cream, red, and black.

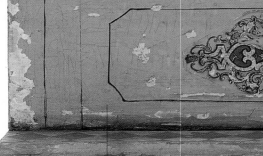

Ornate gilded panels typical of Christian Hacker houses and room sets.

English words suggest shop was made for export.

THE FACADE AND INTERIOR
Only a glimpse of the shop interior can be seen from the outside. The original contents, and the diamond-patterned paper on the floor and walls, have not suffered as much damage as the typical Hacker paintwork and decorated panels on the facade.

Wooden-handled meat cleaver.

One of several metal knives.

Painted metal bucket.

BUTCHER'S EQUIPMENT
(ABOVE) The metal meat cleaver was designed to hang from a nail, while the painted metal bucket was provided to stand under uncut hanging carcasses.

Facade is decorated with gilded frieze.

Metal hinge on cash booth door.

CASH BOOTH *(ABOVE)*
This booth has a carved fascia board above the door and a hinged front, which gives access to a seat behind the window counter. The "Cash" sign above the window is made of paper.

Butcher wears German-style clothes including smock, baggy trousers, gaiters, and cap.

Wooden lattice gate across entrance has metal handle and hinges.

TIN BATHROOM
German; c.1920s

U NLIKE A FULLY EQUIPPED TOY KITCHEN, which fascinates by its wealth of everyday items, the bathroom has few contents and little decoration. Yet it has proved a popular toy for generations of children, especially when, as in this example, water is available "on tap." This apparently simple little painted metal room set hides a complex system of working faucets and drains. The pump draws water into tanks on the back walls, and from these the bath and basin are filled, the toilet is flushed, and the shower supplied.

This example is relatively well appointed, with a gilded mirror, toilet-paper holder, towel racks, fluffy towels, and a matching bathmat; there is even a bath thermometer.

Any fears that too many cold baths might have removed the doll's coloring and frozen her stiff are ill-founded; little figures such as this were always made of glazed white ceramic.

Round, gilt-framed mirror suspended from hook on side wall.

Faucet swivels to control water supply.

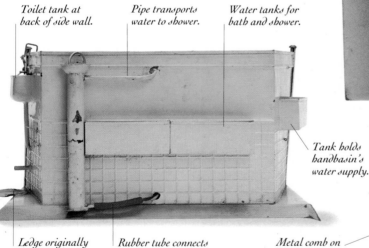

Toilet tank at back of side wall.

Pipe transports water to shower.

Water tanks for bath and shower.

Tank holds handbasin's water supply.

Ledge originally held waste-water container.

Rubber tube connects bath's drainage pipe to pump.

Metal comb on handbasin.

13in (33cm)

7½in (19cm)

Painted tin bathroom; "plumbed-in" water supply.

PLUMBING SYSTEM *(ABOVE)*
After the appropriate faucet is turned on, water from a tank on the back wall is pumped into the bath or showerhead by pulling the ring on top of the pump up and down. Waste is then returned from the bath to the system via a waste pipe.

THE BATHROOM

The lower walls in this simple tin bathroom have a stamped tile pattern, while the upper walls are painted blue with gilt picture rail and dado rail. The bath, the toilet, and the sink are tin. The faucets, towel racks, and showerhead are brass.

Lever mechanism for flushing toilet.

Pipe from cistern to toilet bowl.

Raised tile pattern stamped into sheets of tin.

Ring of plunger pulled up and down to pump water.

Waste pipe from toilet bowl.

TOILET CISTERN *(LEFT)*

The toilet has a cistern behind the right side wall. The "flush" was operated by a system of levers from the cistern to a ring that once hung beside the toilet. A container originally stood on the ledge under the cistern to collect waste water.

WASHINGTON DOLLS' HOUSE & TOY MUSEUM

Round, perforated metal showerhead.

Bathroom thermometer.

COMMERCIALLY MADE DOLLS' HOUSES

*During the nineteenth century, the concept of miniature houses changed as they began
to be commercially produced in quantity, and the ornamental "baby houses" of adult collectors
evolved into "dolls' houses" intended as childrens' playthings. In the mid-twentieth century
another phase began: adults as well as children began to enjoy the charms of modern dolls'
houses, and antique playthings were increasingly sought by collectors.*

RESEARCH BY VIVIEN GREENE, the English authority on dolls' houses, has revealed that the famous London toy seller Bellamy advertised a list of "toys" for adults and children on his December 1762 trade card: "Baby-houses, with all Sorts of Furniture at the lowest Price. Wholesale and Retail." This suggests that some commercially produced dolls' houses were made for children in England earlier than is usually supposed. From the middle of the nineteenth century, however, dolls' houses as playthings were certainly being manufactured in large quantities, mainly by German and English firms.

As Dickens vividly illustrates in his portrayal of Caleb, the toy maker in *The Cricket on the Hearth*, most English dolls' houses in the mid-nineteenth century were produced at home by craftsmen who sold their houses wholesale to shops. If Caleb is a typical example (and Dickens is generally regarded as a reliable reporter), these craftsmen produced a prodigious variety of houses: "... suburban tenements for dolls of moderate means; kitchens and single apartments for dolls of the lowest classes; capital town residences for dolls of high estate ... some already furnished according to estimate ... others could be filled at a moment's notice, from whole shelves of chairs and tables, sofas, bedsteads, and upholstery."

FRENCH SEASIDE VILLAS *(LEFT)*
Mon Repos (far left and pp.80–81) *is a very decorative dolls' house with two lavishly wall-papered rooms. The house next to it is a later, plainer, and obviously cheaper version. It, too, has steps to a porticoed front door, a door to a balcony, and a mock attic window, but its interior walls are not wallpapered.*

and Converse. Dolls' houses never achieved as much popularity in the Mediterranean countries as they did in the northern regions. Museums in Denmark, Norway, and Sweden contain several interesting nineteenth-century dolls' houses; some of these were imported from Germany, but others were made, and at least partially furnished, in Scandinavia. Several of the most famous modern dolls' house and miniature furniture manufacturers are Scandinavian: products from the Swedish firm Lundby are distributed throughout the world, and pieces by Brio (also Swedish) and the Danish firm Hanse, which reflect current fashions and styles, attract adults as well as children.

— FAMOUS NAMES —

For nearly two centuries, however, it was the German and British manufacturers, joined later by American firms, who produced most of the dolls' houses, furniture, and accessories that are

1914 ENGLISH COTTAGE
(ABOVE) This unusual papier-mâché and wood cottage was commercially made, according to its label, by Mrs. Florence Callcott. It is open-backed, with a hinged, painted door and windows, and internal staircase.

DOLLY'S PLAY HOUSE
(RIGHT) McLoughlin Bros of New York produced this lavishly decorated, printed-paper-covered folding dolls' house from c.1884 to 1903 in brighter colors than those suggested by the box lid.

Well into the twentieth century, many British dolls' house manufacturers and retailers were based in London, as were the warehouses for imported dolls' houses, which came mainly from Germany. London children were well served: Silber & Fleming (manufacturers and importers) and Cremer (importer and toy shop); the stalls in the Lawther Arcade and Morrell's famous shop in the Burlington Arcade; Gamages and Whiteleys department stores – these are just some of the names that make today's dolls' house collectors long for the loan of a time machine.

During the nineteenth century, English and German dolls' houses were being exported to the United States, where they were advertised in the catalogs of stores such as Sears, Roebuck and F.A.O. Schwarz along with best-selling lines from American manufacturers like Bliss, Schoenhut, McLoughlin,

BLISS FURNITURE (*RIGHT*)
From c.1888 until 1901 R. Bliss of Pawtucket, Rhode Island, advertised dolls' house furniture packed "in strong pasteboard boxes" with "beautifully lithographed labels." This set of lithographed parlor furniture contains a piano, table, sofa, and chairs. Bliss made other similar sets, including one of bedroom furniture.

SILBER & FLEMING DOLLS' HOUSE
(*BELOW*) *The dolls' houses produced by this c.1850–1900 London manufacturer and importer ranged from small two-room villas to six-room mansions with staircases. Most were "box backs" with front-opening facades and painted stone and brickwork. Countless Victorian nurseries possessed a variation of this typical best-selling design.*

now the much-prized possessions of contemporary collectors. Dolls' houses made by Moritz Gottschalk (1865–1939) and Christian Hacker (1870–1914); pressed-tin furniture, painted to resemble wood, by Rock & Graner (1825–1904); "Waltershausen" imitation inlaid rosewood pieces by Schneegas (1830s–1940); and filigree metal furniture made by Schweitzer (founded in 1796 and still in production) are all held in high regard and command correspondingly high prices. The same may be said about the tinplate furniture made by the English firm Evans & Cartwright (1800–80) and the gilded metal pieces, which often included "novelty" needlecases in the shape of miniature chairs, by Avery & Sons (*c.*1860s).

Even twentieth-century dolls' houses, such as those made by Lines (1919–71), and furnished by Elgin (1919–26) or Barton (1945–84), are seen by some as collectors' items in the 1990s.

— HOUSING PREFERENCES —

The English have traditionally chosen houses rather than room sets, attracted by their realistic facades. To a large extent, dolls' houses have been favored in the United States also. In Europe, however, and especially in France and Germany, room settings have usually been preferred.

Most nineteenth-century dolls' houses in the middle or upper price range were made of wood, painted to resemble brick and stone, but some excellent paper and cardboard models were also produced; these became particularly popular in

1928 CARDBOARD HOUSES *(LEFT)*
Cheap cardboard dolls' houses were popular in the United States during the 1920s. Sears, Roebuck's 1928 catalog offered a six-room house and a bungalow in two sizes.

the United States toward the end of the nineteenth century. By 1910, various American manufacturers were producing very well-printed designs; probably the most famous name was that of McLoughlin Brothers *(see pp.86–87)*, whose lines of printed, folding houses were also exported to the United Kingdom.

Before the introduction of plastic, tin or a heavier sheet metal was used for dolls' houses, room settings, and furniture. In the United States, as early as 1869, Louis Marx, Mettoy, and several lesser known firms were producing attractive,

brightly lithographed tinplate buildings. Today, plastic materials are used extensively by modern manufacturers. Two current best-sellers are the Playmobil *c.*1900-style mansion, which is made entirely from brightly colored, injection-molded plastic, and the open-fronted houses, made by the Swedish firm Lundby, which are constructed from a mixture of plastic, fiberboard, and wood.

Houses supplied in kit form are also popular. A British firm, Hobbies of Dereham, has provided such plans and materials for decades *(see pp.94–95)*. Books of printed paper and cardboard houses, which have only to be cut out and glued or slotted together, also sell well. Several have been made with printed interior rooms, and some have furniture printed on the walls. One ingenious version, described as a "carousel pop-up book house," is illustrated on page 112.

But even in these plastic-dominated days, painted wood is still the favorite material for Caleb's successors – those who make the dolls' houses now sold in specialty stores, and are designed for children or adults to furnish – if not at "the lowest prices" as advertised by Bellamy in 1762, still "with all Sorts of Furniture."

SCHOENHUT ROOM *(LEFT)*
This room is from a house made by Schoenhut of Philadelphia. The walls are simply painted with stenciled friezes and cutout doorways. Its dolls and furniture are recent additions.

TWINKY DOLLS *(ABOVE)*
In 1964 the American firm Grandmother Stover advertised these jointed plastic dolls' house dolls, all painted and dressed by Ethel Strong, who commissioned the dolls from a molder.

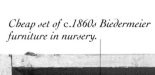

No. 12

— Possibly English or German; c.1870s —

BOX-BACK DOLLS' HOUSES, like the one featured here, were to be found in many late-nineteenth-century nurseries, as such dolls' houses were being commercially produced at that time. But because this house has no maker's mark or distinguishing feature, and because so many models like it were being made in England and Germany at this period, it is difficult to be sure of the house's exact origins.

Although the exterior of No. 12 is plain, apart from its balconies and decorative brickwork, the interior displays genuine 1870s patterned wallpapers, carpets, and furnishings (mostly German), a plethora of pictures and ornaments, and an "Upstairs, Downstairs" household of 11 doll inhabitants. "No. 12," incidentally, was discovered painted on the front door of the house.

Painted wooden quoining.

Decorative "brick" lintels painted over window.

Ornate metal balcony, painted maroon and gold.

Balusters nailed to wooden floor and top rail.

Cream-painted window ledge.

Steps nailed to front door.

Painted wooden door.

46in (117cm)

38½in (98cm)

Box-back house; hinged two-section front opening.

THE FACADE
The metal balconies and "brick" lintels above the windows relieve the plain facade of this simple box-back house, which has no other features on the back or sides. Each of the 14 glazed windows has one painted glazing bar and a small wooden window ledge.

Cheap set of c.1860s Biedermeier furniture in nursery.

Original metal fireplace in nursery.

Wooden kitchen dresser attached to side wall.

Kitchen table has long drawer and hinged side extensions.

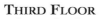

Very thick, shiny, embossed and gilded paper.

Chimney extends through all floors.

Blocked-in fireplace below mantelpiece in maids' room.

THIRD FLOOR

A brass fender guards the fire in the nursery *(left)*, where a child is playing. The room is furnished with simple wooden furniture, as is the maids' room *(right)*, which also contains a plain tin hip bath.

China basin and ewer on wooden washstand.

SECOND FLOOR

The drawing room *(right)* and bedroom *(left)* are furnished in Victorian style with a wealth of pictures, mirrors, ornaments, and lamps, as well as Waltershausen furniture. Next to the bed is a set of steps and a chamber pot.

Candle sconces and chandeliers provide lighting.

Oriental carved ivory elephant candle holder.

Chandelier raised and lowered by pulley and chain.

Gilt-framed prints on side walls.

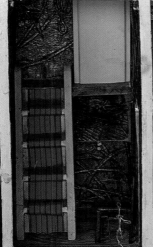

FIRST FLOOR

Adjacent to the hall are the kitchen *(left)*, with its original black metal kitchen stove, and the dining room *(right)*, which is fashionably decorated in crimson and gilt and furnished with a set of Waltershausen furniture, a "marble" fireplace, and gilt-framed portraits.

Removable stairs with steep steps.

1870s painted wallpaper provides "tiles" in hall.

Dining room carpet made from part of wool paisley shawl.

Portraits are miniatures of owner's ancestors.

Flocked panels on dado.

REALISTIC INTERIOR

ONLY THE FIREPLACES, including the kitchen stove, and stairs in No. 12 are original; everything else, although of the correct period, has been collected for the house. In the main rooms, most of the furniture is Waltershausen "rosewood," but the house contains English silver, copper, and brass items, and a few oriental pieces. The drawing room curtains are Chinese embroidered panels, hung when the house was restored some years ago by the present owner.

WOODEN WASHTUB (*BELOW*)
The washtub is reinforced with metal hoops; the washboard is also of wood and metal.

English "iron" kettle with removable lid.

Hot-water faucet on boiler.

Red-painted metal coal bucket.

English copper fish kettle.

Toweling and flannel frequently used in Victorian households.

Gridiron made of heavy "iron."

Typical mid-19th-century pressed-metal kitchen stove.

FIRE IRONS (*LEFT*)
The heavy gridiron usually hangs on the wall beside the stove; the other implements in this set of heavy metal kitchen fire irons rest in the hearth.

KITCHEN STOVE (*ABOVE*)
An English silver coffeepot and heavy kettle stand on the stove, which has a hot oven above a slow one on the left; the fire also heats water in a boiler on the right. Both the grate and the red coal bucket contain real coal.

Three-pronged "iron" fork.

Heavy "iron" tongs are not hinged.

Waltershausen sofa with decorative "ivory" arm panels.

Fine decorative lacquerwork on both interior and exterior.

Metal handle on removable drawer.

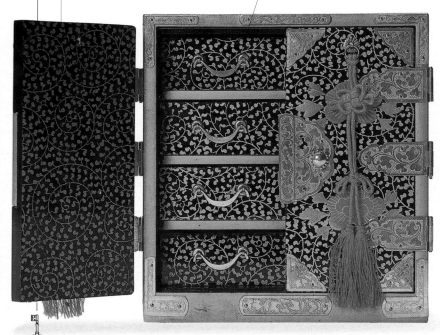

LACQUER CHEST (*LEFT*)
This elaborate chest of drawers, part of an antique Japanese Hina Matsuri set, has decorative silk tassels and silver-plated panels.

WALTERSHAUSEN SOFA
(*ABOVE*) The sofa is upholstered in rose pink velvet and trimmed with gold and fringed braid. The back is covered with green paper.

GERMAN BISQUE DOLLS

ALL THE DOLLS in this house, both family and staff, are medium-quality white bisques with tinted cheeks and painted features. Except for the baby, whose curls are painted, the dolls have mohair wigs. The three children are all-bisque dolls, wire-jointed at the hips and shoulders. The adults have soft bodies, upper arms, and legs, stitch-jointed, with bisque shoulder-heads, hands, and feet.

THE FAMILY (RIGHT)

The No. 12 family, with four children, is small by Victorian standards, but they have all been dressed in appropriate 1870s-style clothing, made from old fabrics, in designs copied from contemporary fashion plates.

THE STAFF (BELOW)

The baby of the family is shown here with Nanny and the other staff. Cook and the housemaid seem anxious about the coachman's empty tankard.

Mama wears velvet and satin dress.

Younger son dressed in early version of sailor suit.

Papa reclines in green leather armchair.

Elder son's wig is made of red mohair.

All-bisque doll with wire-jointed arms and legs.

Daughter wears fashionable dress with bustle bow.

Cavalier King Charles spaniel made of bisque.

Cook wears full-skirted dress, white apron, and cap.

Coachman dressed in full livery, including cockaded hat.

Housemaid wears print dress and old-fashioned apron.

Bisque family pet is probably a Persian cat.

Baby wears white silk and lace gown.

Nanny wears traditional cap with lappets and blue dress.

Wooden bottle and glass tankard.

Wickerwork cradle still has original trimming and rockers.

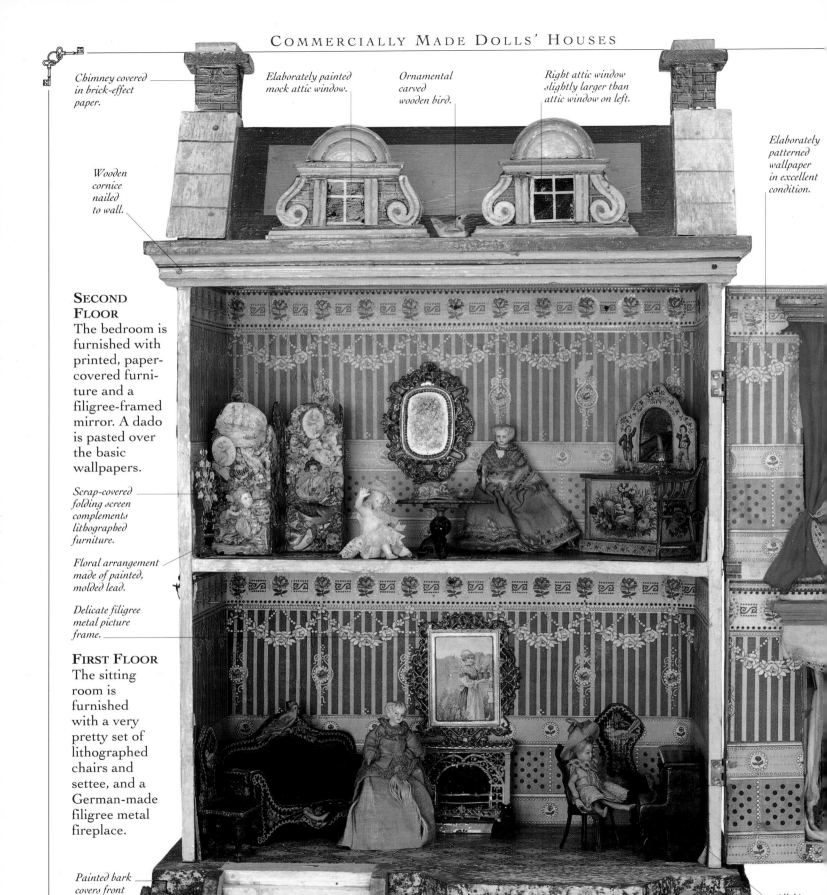

Chimney covered in brick-effect paper.

Elaborately painted mock attic window.

Ornamental carved wooden bird.

Right attic window slightly larger than attic window on left.

Elaborately patterned wallpaper in excellent condition.

Wooden cornice nailed to wall.

SECOND FLOOR

The bedroom is furnished with printed, paper-covered furniture and a filigree-framed mirror. A dado is pasted over the basic wallpapers.

Scrap-covered folding screen complements lithographed furniture.

Floral arrangement made of painted, molded lead.

Delicate filigree metal picture frame.

FIRST FLOOR

The sitting room is furnished with a very pretty set of lithographed chairs and settee, and a German-made filigree metal fireplace.

Painted bark covers front and sides of base, suggesting rock.

All-bisque child doll seated at wooden piano.

MON REPOS

Probably German; c.1890s–1900s

THE STYLE OF THIS DELIGHTFUL small house has been described as resembling that of a late-nineteenth-century French seaside villa. The facade suggests a more spacious interior than the house actually possesses: there are just two rooms, without even a staircase between them. The interior splendor is confined to the unexpectedly elaborate wallpapers – red and green versions of the same pattern. Both rooms have wooden cornices, draped curtains, and the same detailed, patterned, printed paper floor covering; the inner surfaces of the doors are surprisingly crude. The windows are very attractive: those in the attic are ornately painted, and the glazed lower ones are equipped with venetian blinds. Bark, representing rock, has been nailed to the deep base.

Backing of venetian blinds behind curtains.

Lace-edged curtains looped back with metal hooks.

Brick-effect paper from facade folded around edge.

Inner surface of door crudely finished.

Lace-trimmed cotton curtains at glazed bay window.

Door hinged to open inward.

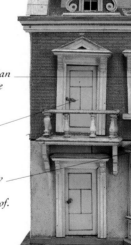

Unusual orange-painted roof with brown border.

Green paper venetian blinds pasted inside windows.

Door opens onto balcony with balustrade.

Roof of bay window painted in style similar to main roof.

Steep flight of painted wooden steps.

THE FACADE
Although German dolls' house manufacturers were influenced by contemporary styles of architecture, they did not confine themselves to making only miniature replicas. Mon Repos bears no manufacturer's mark, but it is probably one of the many German dolls' houses that were designed to appeal to a specific export market.

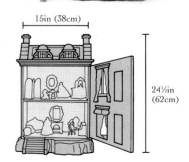

15in (38cm)

24½in (62cm)

Painted and papered wood; hinged front opening.

HACKER HOUSE

— *Made in Germany; c.1890s* —

THE NUREMBERG FIRM Christian Hacker was founded in the 1870s, but this particular house was probably made nearer the turn of the century. It is an unusual version of a design that was usually constructed with only two floors. The different decoration of the third floor, which is the only one with side bay windows, suggests that this may have been a later addition – a relatively easy alteration, as the roof was designed to be removable. However, the manufacturer did produce many variations of certain basic designs.

Some original floor papers remain and the wallpaper in all five rooms is old, although it was added after the house was purchased. There are interior doors, but no staircase; the windows are glazed and the front doors are hinged to open.

House is of simple "box on box" construction.

Three-paned bay window on side wall of top floor.

Printed paper decoration below and above top window.

Decorative transfer on panel.

Rock & Graner tin-plate chaise longue covered in silk.

Door originally opened onto balcony.

Cotton blind inside window.

Dado of dark wood-grain-effect paper.

Typical Christian Hacker line decoration.

Hutch shelving lacks original base section.

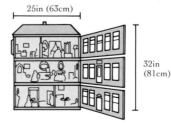

25in (63cm)

32in (81cm)

Wooden structure; three hinged facade sections.

THE FACADE

Each of the floors of this house has a separate hinged facade section. Ornamental panels on the first two floors are transfers, but the third floor has printed paper decorations. The door on the second floor indicates that the house once had a balcony.

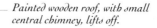

Painted wooden roof, with small
central chimney, lifts off.

Hinges for top-floor opening facade
smaller than those on other two
floors, suggesting this is an addition.

Decorative gold braid
valance surmounts
lace curtains.

Photograph of Queen
Alexandra, wife of
British monarch
Edward VII, in
decorative metal
frame.

Cane cradle lacks
original rockers.

Child's portrait
in gilded pressed-
metal frame.

Larger hinges used on
front opening sections
of lower floors.

Fashionably attired
doll wears blue
dress with train.

Side panels and
front of sideboard
richly decorated.

Typically dark but
lavishly patterned late-
nineteenth-century
wallpaper.

Painted bronze
roses in flowerpot.

Pressed-tin arm-
chair upholstered
in red velvet.

Original geometrically
patterned floor paper.

THIRD FLOOR
Both rooms on this floor are
arranged as bedrooms, with
a connecting door. In each
room is a side bay window
with white lace curtains
and a gold braid valance.
Although most of the furniture is Waltershausen, the
most interesting item is the
Rock & Graner half-tester
bed in the smaller room on
the left. Equally charming,
but less rare, are the pink
and black painted tin bath
set and the cane cradle in
the larger bedroom *(right)*.

SECOND FLOOR
The drawing room occupies
this entire floor; it has no
side windows, doors, or
access to other floors. The
room is handsomely furnished with a lavishly decorated
suite of chromolithographed
pieces and a Rock & Graner
chaise longue upholstered
in purple silk. On the chaise
longue is a miniature copy
of *Weldon's Ladies' Journal*.

FIRST FLOOR
A brightly painted mantelpiece surrounds the original
tinplate stove in the kitchen
(left) – the larger of the two
rooms on the first floor. The
remaining section of the
wooden dresser is laden with
china, "silver," and food. A
footman has just come into
the kitchen from the somber,
but elaborately decorated,
dining room next door.

GERMAN FURNISHINGS

THE CHRISTIAN HACKER HOUSE contains many excellent examples of different types of mid- to late-nineteenth-century dolls' house furniture; the chromolithographed pieces in the drawing room are particularly eye-catching, while the Rock & Graner chaise longue, pedestal table, and small half-tester bed, draped with green curtains, are of great interest to collectors. Other unusual items include the pressed-tin armchair, which is upholstered in red velvet. The work of Waltershausen toy makers is well represented, the piano in the drawing room being noteworthy.

Elegant wooden chair covered in chromolithographed paper.

Sideboard covered in decorated paper panels.

Cupid design popular in 1880s.

Fireplace has painted coal, alight and smoking.

Chair upholstered in pink velvet, edged with gilt paper braid.

FIREPLACE *(LEFT)*
The gilded, pierced metal ornamentation, enhanced by a black fire back with painted fire effect, made this tiny fireplace a best-seller.

Door of sideboard hinged to open.

Hinged, slightly curved door.

HUTCH *(BELOW)*
It is likely that this is the top section of the hutch shelving and the base is now missing. The contents of the shelves were probably all made in Thuringia (but the portrait is of the British monarch Edward VII).

DECORATIVE FURNITURE *(ABOVE)* The chair and pair of sideboards are excellent examples of plain wooden items that have been transformed by the application of chromolithographed paper.

Photograph in ornate metal frame.

Top section of painted wooden kitchen hutch.

Cream and brown pottery pitcher.

Wooden bowl made in Germany.

Typical design for small mass-produced pitchers.

Painted plaster orange on wooden plate.

Painted, molded plaster sandwiches on plate.

Stack of painted wooden plates.

German-made soft metal vase.

Shaped side panels of typical Hacker design.

Pierced tin tray with matching glass holders.

WALTERSHAUSEN FURNITURE (BELOW)

Waltershausen, in Thuringia, was a center of wooden toy making. The bureau and chest of drawers were made by Schneegas, a local firm renowned for its imitation rosewood and gilt furniture.

Painted bronze rose in pot.

Simulated rosewood bureau decorated with gilt transfers.

Silk-covered seat of chair edged with gilt paper braid.

Drawers ornamented with "Gothic" transfers.

China toilet set decorated with "onion pattern" design.

Chest of drawers with marble top, used as washstand.

Piano has reversed key coloring.

Decorative pink panel of upright piano edged with gilt paper.

NINETEENTH-CENTURY GERMAN LADIES

FIVE GERMAN DOLLS' HOUSE DOLLS are shown in the Christian Hacker house, but the china-headed doll with the fashionable hat may be a visitor. Although it is likely that the dolls were all dressed after purchase, the costumes of the two from the drawing room (left and right, below) have been elaborately trimmed and pleated with considerable skill. The identical bisque-headed dolls have finely molded hairstyles; the footman and visitor are china-headed dolls with black hair. All the dolls have soft stitch-jointed bodies with bisque lower arms and legs, a type that was popular from c.1870 until 1890.

Elaborately molded bisque hairstyle.

Doll has bisque head and limbs and soft body.

Dress based on mid-1870s English style.

Extensively pleated homemade dress.

Identical twin of other bisque-headed example (left).

China-headed doll with shiny black-painted hair.

Plain tailored outfit with velvet trimming.

Fashionable hat glued to doll's head.

Checked and embroidered dress with elaborately pleated train.

THE PRETTY VILLAGE

American; produced by McLoughlin Brothers, New York, in 1897

BEST KNOWN FOR the fine color printing of its larger and heavier cardboard dolls' houses, all with sumptuously decorated interiors, McLoughlin Brothers first produced The Pretty Village in 1897. It proved to be extremely popular, and several different editions were printed over a number of years. All editions were sold in large boxes with attractive, colorful pictures on the lids *(see p.73)*.

Constructing the village was simple: you had to cut out a building, fold and glue the tabs in place, and then position the finished product on the planned base (for which directions were given) or design a village layout to your own specifications.

Although these buildings are small and printed only on the exterior, children derived hours of pleasure from making them and then planning the layout. The village shown here has eight houses and includes a log cabin, a school, a fire station, a blacksmith's shop, a boathouse, and a photographer's studio. Sadly, it has none of the freestanding cut-out figures found in some sets.

COTTAGE *(ABOVE)*
The child in this cottage, with its red-tiled roof, is happy and industrious, like all the children in The Pretty Village.

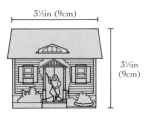

3½in (9cm)

3½in (9cm)

No access to interior; details printed in full color on cardboard.

CLAPBOARD HOUSE *(BELOW)* This pretty clapboard house has a shingled gable, two balconies, and a veranda.

Child fishes alongside "Friendship Boat Club" boathouse.

BOATHOUSE *(BELOW)*
The layout plan of this building includes a waterfront.

GREENHOUSE *(BELOW)*
This charming greenhouse, well stocked with colorful and tropical plants, belongs to M.A. Flower the Florist.

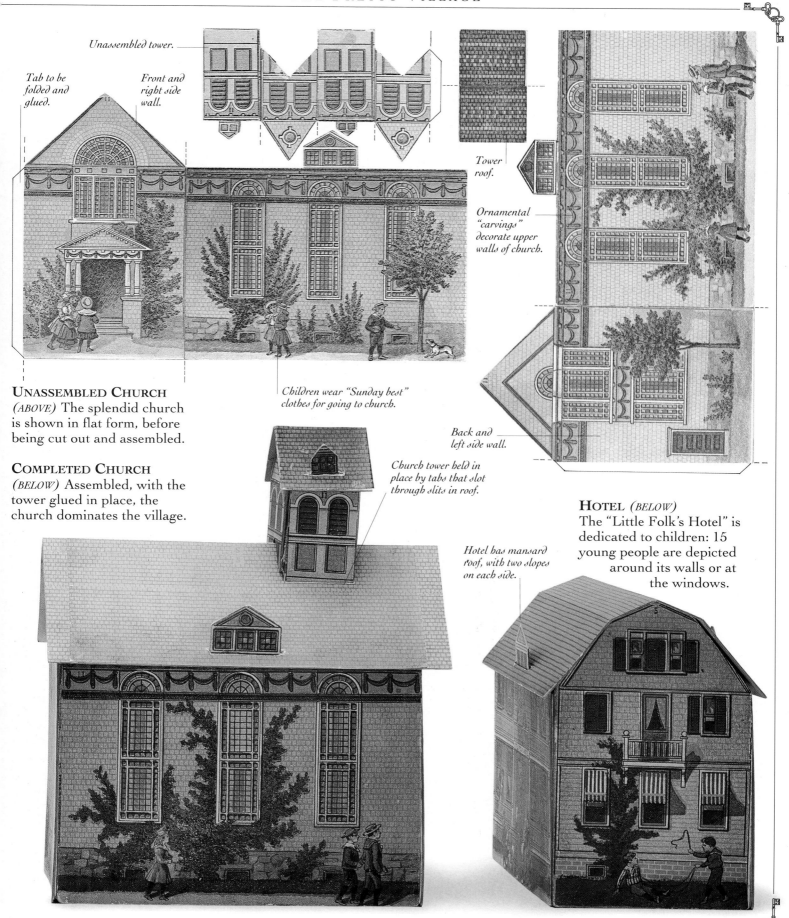

Unassembled tower.

Tab to be folded and glued.

Front and right side wall.

Tower roof.

Ornamental "carvings" decorate upper walls of church.

UNASSEMBLED CHURCH
(ABOVE) The splendid church is shown in flat form, before being cut out and assembled.

COMPLETED CHURCH
(BELOW) Assembled, with the tower glued in place, the church dominates the village.

Children wear "Sunday best" clothes for going to church.

Back and left side wall.

Church tower held in place by tabs that slot through slits in roof.

HOTEL *(BELOW)*
The "Little Folk's Hotel" is dedicated to children: 15 young people are depicted around its walls or at the windows.

Hotel has mansard roof, with two slopes on each side.

CANOE AND DOG *(ABOVE)*
The canoe is made of birch bark stitched to framework. The hunting hound has a well-molded, skin-covered body with painted features.

SECOND FLOOR
Only one upstairs room is visible at the back, but there is a side attic with an open window, accessible when the hinged roof is lifted up.

FIRST FLOOR
Both the main room and the kitchen have hinged doors and open windows. The plainly furnished rooms have decorative rugs on the floor.

TRIPOD AND POT *(BELOW)*
Rolled birch-bark shavings provide the "logs" for this campfire. A cooking pot hangs from the tripod; both are made of blackwood.

Handmade canoe and wooden paddle.

Lithographed mounted stag's head.

Hinged side attic roof section.

Unglazed window opening.

Steeply pitched roof has painted shingle effect.

Main roof section attached to walls of house.

Simple bentwood furniture.

Small plastic bulldog.

Main room covered with wood-grain-effect paper.

Wooden paddle propped against wall.

Cooking pot suspended from tripod.

Printed raccoon-skin design on flannel rug.

Doll wearing checked woolen dress has bisque head and limbs.

Woven basket contains birch-bark "logs."

ADIRONDACK COTTAGE

American; probably made by Bliss of Pawtucket, Rhode Island, in 1904

Carved wooden handle with lithographed American Indian figurehead.

THE NATIONAL NOVELTY CORPORATION was selling the "Adirondack Cottage novel dolls' house" in 1904, but no mention was made in its advertisements of the manufacturer's name. However, given the quality of construction and the materials used (lithographed paper-covered wood) and Bliss's later references to its production of "cabins," the most likely contender seems to be Bliss of Pawtucket, Rhode Island – at that time a member of the National Novelty Corporation.

The exterior walls are covered in lithographed log-patterned paper, the interior walls with a wood finish, while the base has a checkered blackwood top with stone-and-mortar sides. The lithographed stags' heads on the gables are purely decorative, but the American Indian figurehead on the side attic roof acts as a handle. Although the window openings are unglazed, two lithographed windows on the right side wall suggest glazing, with green blinds downstairs and frilly curtains upstairs. The doors are plain, but the balcony and gable have decorative features. The design that was originally advertised had more ornamental features, including a papered stone-effect chimney.

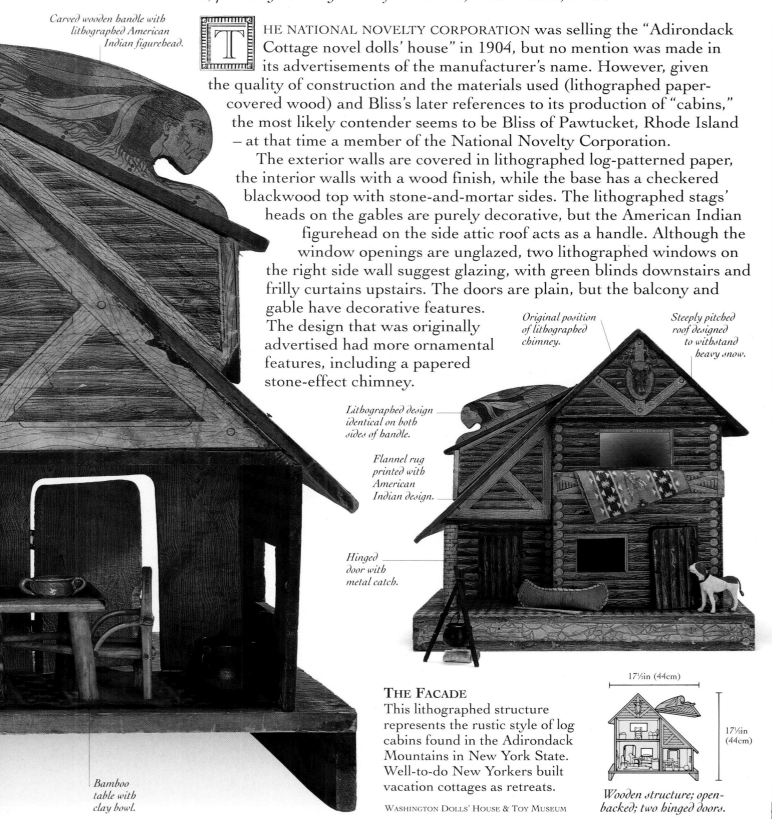

Original position of lithographed chimney.

Steeply pitched roof designed to withstand heavy snow.

Lithographed design identical on both sides of handle.

Flannel rug printed with American Indian design.

Hinged door with metal catch.

Bamboo table with clay bowl.

THE FACADE
This lithographed structure represents the rustic style of log cabins found in the Adirondack Mountains in New York State. Well-to-do New Yorkers built vacation cottages as retreats.

WASHINGTON DOLLS' HOUSE & TOY MUSEUM

17½in (44cm)

17½in (44cm)

Wooden structure; open-backed; two hinged doors.

BLISS HOUSE

American; made by Bliss of Pawtucket; c.1904

RUFUS BLISS ESTABLISHED the Bliss Manufacturing Company in 1832 to make wooden piano screws. He retired in 1863, and the firm later started manufacturing toys. Between *c.*1890 and 1914, it produced the dolls' houses that made the Bliss name famous. From 1903 until 1907 Bliss and other leading American toy makers traded together as the National Novelty Corporation; during these years many Bliss houses were sold by the corporation. Bliss lines continued in production despite a later takeover, and this particular design was still selling in 1920, confirming not only its popularity but also the firm's reputation for well-made products, a point that Bliss had always emphasized when advertising.

In addition to dolls' houses (designs ranged from log cabins to suburban residences), Bliss also produced stables, shops, warehouses, and even fire stations and a fort. All these toys, like the dolls' houses, were constructed of wood covered with colorful lithographed paper.

SECOND FLOOR
Despite its elaborate facade, the house has a simple interior with only one main room on each floor, and no staircase. The out-of-scale wallpaper marks this house as a later Bliss model, and contrasts vividly with the well-proportioned lithographed exterior.

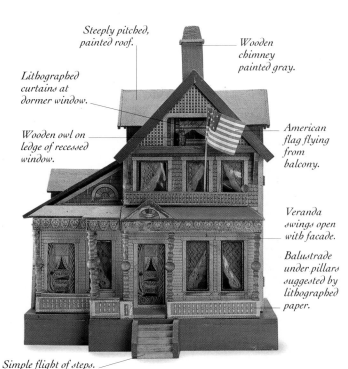

Steeply pitched, painted roof.

Wooden chimney painted gray.

Lithographed curtains at dormer window.

Wooden owl on ledge of recessed window.

American flag flying from balcony.

Veranda swings open with facade.

Balustrade under pillars suggested by lithographed paper.

Simple flight of steps.

6in (15cm)

9in (23cm)

Lithograph-covered wood; hinged front and side wall.

Lithographed semicircular window in shingled roof.

LOGO (ABOVE)
A Bliss logo appears twice on this house: on the lower panel of the front door and on the porch pediment.

FIRST FLOOR
The front door opens into the main room, furnished with only two items. An interior door leads to the kitchen, which also has a side entrance.

THE FACADE
Bliss houses are renowned for the quality and detail of their lithographed exterior designs. This model, with its roofed veranda, recessed mock upper-floor window, and five-dormered roof, presents a complex facade that belies the simple interior.

Kitchen door hinged to open inward.

Left wall of ground floor hinged to open.

Bisque-headed doll wears beige double-breasted suit.

No access to attic space, although lithographed window on facade suggests presence of room there.

Central wooden chimney.

Out-of-scale wallpaper, used on later Bliss houses.

Projecting balcony roof matches steeply pitched house roof.

Wooden-framed settee covered in lithographed paper.

Turned wooden leg.

Three-legged chair with lithographed seat and back.

PARLOR FURNITURE (*ABOVE*) These two pieces are from a set of Bliss wooden furniture decorated with lithographed paper; the set includes four chairs, a piano, and a settee.

Lithographed balustraded balcony projects over roof of veranda.

Net curtains drape windows.

Ornamental turned wooden pillar.

Pressed-tin suitcase.

Deep base typical of Bliss house design.

WASHINGTON DOLLS' HOUSE & TOY MUSEUM

THE INTERIOR

The four rooms are all papered with colorful modern patterns, with the additional attraction of trompe l'oeil fireplaces and doorways – a rather unexpected bonus in what seems, from the outside, to be a charming but fairly simple little bungalow. The wooden staircase leads to two low-ceilinged attics.

Wooden chimney attached to rear roof section.

Glazed window in attic.

Side of house hinged to open.

Pressed cardboard furniture by Moritz Gottschalk.

Trompe l'oeil bathroom and doorway.

Wooden staircase leads to attic.

Trompe l'oeil fireplace in hall.

SCHOENHUT BUNGALOW

American; made by A. Schoenhut of Philadelphia; 1917

ALBERT SCHOENHUT left Germany for the United States in 1867 at the age of 17. He was from a toy-making family in Wurttemberg and continued the family tradition by founding a toy-making company in Philadelphia, Pennsylvania, in 1872. In 1917, when the firm was already well known for wooden dolls, circuses, and toy musical instruments, it introduced a new line, which was advertised as "High-class Dolls' Houses and Bungalows."

Schoenhut's miniature bungalows, which echoed a popular contemporary style of residence, became best-sellers. Unlike today's dolls' house manufacturers, the firm used architectural trends to advantage, emphasizing "the most modern style of paper hanging" in lithographed interiors, with many trompe l'oeil effects. This style changed in the mid-1920s when Schoenhut began to produce houses with shutters and window boxes on plain exterior walls, and no trompe l'oeil effects inside. Schoenhut toys have always been popular with children, and collectors today seem equally enthusiastic.

Compressed cardboard roof embossed and painted to resemble shingles.

Hinged ridge of front roof section.

Lace curtains at attic window.

Painted wooden window frame around glazed window.

Real staircase made of wood.

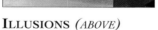

ILLUSIONS *(ABOVE)*
"An illusion of a house full of fine rooms" was promised by Schoenhut's catalog, and fulfilled by this trompe l'oeil image of a room beyond the doorway.

Glass-paneled front door opens inward.

Decorative turned wooden pillar supports veranda.

THE FACADE
The bungalow has glazed windows in an embossed stone-effect front, and a balustraded porch. The red shingled roof has one central dormer window.

Wooden steps set on base.

Painted and embossed stone-effect base.

Label reads, "Manufactured by the A. Schoenhut Co. Philadelphia, PA."

23in (58cm)

20in (50cm)

Front does not open; both sides open; roof tilts back to reveal attic.

HOBBIES HOUSE

English; made from Hobbies dolls' house plans; c.1926

SOME APPARENTLY IDENTICAL dolls' houses may not, in fact, have been commercially made. For many years monthly magazines produced by Hobbies of Dereham, England, have included excellent plans for dolls' houses; once the plans were published many similar dolls' houses were made at home by enthusiasts – often in secret, as a Christmas or birthday surprise for a child.

This particular design was originally meant for a 1:24 scale house, but it was enlarged to a size more suitable for a child. In 1926 Hobbies added furniture plans to its line; the pieces, designed for each room of the dolls' house, were cut from wood with a fretsaw. Later plans included instructions for a garage extension.

Chimney on side wall serves fire below.

Glazed windows, in fretworked frames.

Door and canopy made of varnished wood.

Hinged front door.

Metal press stud represents doorbell.

Painted, curved wooden step.

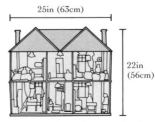

25in (63cm)

22in (56cm)

Paper-covered wood; open-back design; hinged door.

THE FACADE

The exterior of the house is covered with papers supplied by Hobbies: a red-tiled roof, stucco effect on the upper walls, and brickwork on the lower, reflecting the style of houses springing up in the London suburbs at the time.

Hexagonal, wooden-framed mirror above fireplace.

Brass coal scuttle placed beside red brick-effect fireplace.

Wooden bookcase.

Printed roof-tile papers sold by Hobbies.

Block of wood, covered with brick-effect paper, forms chimney.

Gables suggest attic rooms, but roof is firmly attached.

House equipped throughout with working electric lights.

SECOND FLOOR
The second floor has a bedroom, bathroom, and living room, all furnished with *c.*1920s and 1930s items and materials to represent the style of the period. The wooden bedroom furniture is by Elgin, which made dolls' house furniture from 1919 to 1926. A porcelain bath is visible in the central bathroom.

German doll with wool-covered limbs and painted metal head, hands, and feet.

FIRST FLOOR
Both the kitchen *(right)* and the dining room *(left)* have fireplaces attached to a chimney that extends down the end walls of the house. A broom cupboard is built in underneath the stairs.

Tile-effect wallpaper was often used in 1920s kitchens.

1930s metal gas stove made by Taylor & Barrett of London, England.

Well-stocked broom cupboard is set under stairs.

Thin but rigid wall.

Doll, with painted ceramic head, hands, and feet, wears original clothing.

Wooden "Pit-a-Pat" sink with metal faucets, made by E. Lehman & Co.

HAMLEYS HOUSE

English; made by Lines Brothers; c.1929

LINES PRODUCED THIS INNOVATIVE DESIGN, with its imitation thatched roof (earlier models had tiles) in 1929. It is a mixture of styles, with an "olde worlde" thatched roof and beams, and a modern garage incorporated into the structure. Although it became one of Lines' most popular models, to many young owners the lack of a designated kitchen in the house was infuriating, and most garages were probably converted, as in this example. The facade of the house is deceptive, hinting that there is an attic in addition to the garage and usual rooms. In fact, there are only two main rooms, with a small one adjoining the bedroom. No bathroom or kitchen was provided, unless the landing and garage were adapted, as here. The house was strongly built, however, and the additional back opening made placing furniture in the deep main rooms easy. The front door and garage doors are both hinged to open. The house still bears the label indicating that it was made for sale by Hamleys Toyshop, London, England.

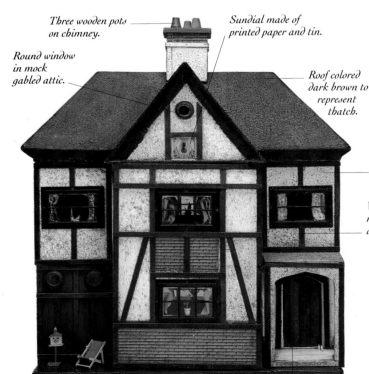

Three wooden pots on chimney.

Sundial made of printed paper and tin.

Round window in mock gabled attic.

Roof colored dark brown to represent thatch.

Walls have white-painted stucco finish.

Wooden "beams" nailed to walls, porch, and garage doors.

Nursery wallpaper was sold in sheets for dolls' houses c.1930.

Tiny bisque doll on nursery table.

SECOND FLOOR
The nursery, bedroom, and bathroom are furnished mainly with wooden items, though the bath is painted metal. The jointed, painted ceramic dolls are German.

FIRST FLOOR
The original first-floor garage was converted into a kitchen, with a doorway cut through to the living room, which is furnished with a 1930s-style, Rexine-covered "Pit-a-Pat" three-piece suite made by E. Lehman & Co.

THE FACADE
Despite its unusual mixture of timbering, stucco, brickwork, and thatch, plus built-in garage, this was one of Lines' best-selling designs. Perhaps adult buyers saw it as reflecting the mock Tudor style of houses being built in the developing English suburbs at the time.

25in (63.5cm)

32in (81cm)

Label reads "Hamleys, 200–202 Regent Street, London W.1."

Wooden door with curved top and three vertical panels.

Facade hinged in four sections; back central section hinged.

Base of chimney is shaped to fit over roof and gable ridgepoles.

Gable with circular window and sundial unique to this model.

DESK *(RIGHT)*
The varnished papier-mâché desk was once a washstand; on it are a glass blotter and ink-stand, bottles of red and black ink, and a pen.

Hand-decorated book covers.

RADIOS *(BELOW)*
Radios were a popular source of home entertain-ment in the 1930s. The simple wooden tabletop radio has printed details, while the floor model (really a pencil sharpener) has paper decoration and dial.

1930s carpet sweeper.

Painted wooden toilet, pedestal sink, and chair.

Molded plastic replica radiogram.

Printed dial and knobs.

Hinged top.

Replica of record made for Queen Mary's Dolls' House.

GRAMOPHONE *(ABOVE RIGHT)*
The metal gramophone has a movable turntable, arm, and handle. The mid-1920s record (in its original "His Master's Voice" sleeve) plays "God Save The King."

CHURCH HILL HOUSE

— *English; made by Lines Brothers in 1939* —

TWENTIETH-CENTURY DOLLS' HOUSE designs generally appear to have been influenced more by the past than by contemporary styles of architecture. However, Lines Brothers did produce several "ultramodern" designs with innovative features, such as movable sunrooms and built-in garages, that were popular at the time. Church Hill House was No. 52 in Lines's 1939 Tri-ang Toys Catalog.

As the London home of the dolls' house owner was prepared for wartime living, so was the dolls' house, which was bought in a sale at Daniel Neale's London shoe store in January 1940 for 8s. 11d. With windows carefully taped over to prevent damage from flying glass, and other air raid precautions, such as blackout curtains, the dolls' house and its family survived the war in London where it still evokes 1940s life in the owner's childhood home.

Metal-framed window was added to balcony to provide a nursery.

THE FACADE
This house reflects the 1930s vogue for flat-roofed houses with simple facades. The typical 1930s color scheme of cream and green, along with the metal window frames, add to its authenticity, as does the air raid shelter.

Movable chimney serves fireplaces below.

Fashionable roof-top sun parlor has open back.

Taped-over windows.

SECOND FLOOR
The bedroom was the only room upstairs until the balcony *(left)* was converted into a nursery. The buckets of sand on the landing and the heavy blackout curtains at the window were typical air raid precautions.

Red and white gingham curtains at kitchen window.

FIRST FLOOR
Until the garage *(left)* was converted into a kitchen, the living room was the only room on this floor. A bathroom was set up under the stairs, where the children's cribs were also placed for protection.

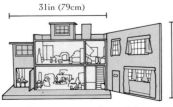

31in (79cm)

23in (58cm)

Wooden structure; hinged front and kitchen section.

Anderson air raid shelter homemade from silvered corrugated paper.

Wooden door with brass fittings opens inward.

Hollow base painted to resemble random paving.

Movable sun-room conceals electric battery.

Typical 1930s-style fireplace.

Air raid warden on fire-watching duty wears yellow "ARP" armband.

Wood and canvas garden chair.

Blackout curtains at side window.

Oil lamp and assorted candles provide emergency lighting during power outages.

Oval wooden dining table and chairs by Pit-a-Pat.

Postwar telephone temporarily replaces missing original.

Childrens' cribs, placed under stairs for protection during air raids, hide bath and toilet in makeshift bathroom.

1940s FURNISHINGS

THE PIT-A-PAT FURNITURE in the living room and kitchen of Church Hill House still has the original price tags attached; the dining room table, for example, cost 1s 3d, while the chairs cost 8d each. Other commercially made items include a metal radio and tea cart, and a Dol-Toi refrigerator. All the wooden bedroom furniture was made by David Davis, the fiancé of the family's cook. The young dolls' house owner made the lace-trimmed crib under the stairs as well as the other nursery furniture.

Handle of painted metal oil stove is movable.

Metal plate rack is adjustable and removable.

Painted metal egg in metal frying pan.

Hinged oven door is removable.

Oval mirror on dressing table has beveled rim.

Brushes and hand mirror have "silver" backs.

OIL HEATER *(ABOVE)*
The metal replica stove heats the bedroom, where the fire screen hides an empty hearth.

GAS STOVE *(ABOVE/RIGHT)*
The gas stove, by Taylor & Barrett, is of white painted metal, with unpainted door and gas burners and a black plate rack – typical 1930s coloring. Because of food rationing, the oven is empty, and only one precious egg is "frying" in the pan.

Pitcher and tumbler set in white-striped Nailsea-style glass.

Varnished wooden tray, one of set of three.

TEA CART *(RIGHT)*
The metal tea cart, with movable wheels and a "brass" handle, is spray-painted in two shades of green. Underneath it is marked "Foreign," indicating that it was imported.

Printed cotton tray cloth is one of set.

DRESSING TABLE *(ABOVE)*
Made from scraps of wood, this varnished dressing table has one drawer that can be pulled out with the aid of two carved wooden handles.

One of set of c.1950s painted metal saucepans with lids.

Metal gelatin molds.

Bead and wire plant in painted wooden flowerpot.

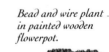

KITCHEN UNITS *(BELOW)*
All three units are made of painted wood; both the sink and washbasin have metal faucets. The refrigerator, from the mid-1940s, still bears its "Dol-Toi" label.

Wooden sink unit with metal faucets and hinged doors.

Wooden washbasin with metal faucets.

WARTIME DOLLS

ALL FOUR DOLLS in this house are German-made, ceramic, and jointed at the shoulders and hips (except for the child in the blue wooden crib, who has no hip joints). They are typical of 1930s dolls, which bridged the gap between the earlier delicate bisque models and the postwar plastic variety. Unlike their bisque forerunners, which were finely molded with painting restricted to the facial features and the hair, these dolls' faces and hands are less well defined, and they are painted all over. Many similar dolls came in sets, dressed as family members or as uniformed staff, but others, like these examples, were bought separately.

One-piece siren suit easily put on and taken off.

FEMALE DOLL *(LEFT)*
This doll originally wore a dress, but she was reclothed in a "siren suit," a practical one-piece garment that was popular during the war (this is a copy of one worn by the owner's mother). She also carries a miniature home-made gas mask.

Miniature replica of cardboard gas mask case with string straps.

Supplies prepared for air raid shelter.

Metal thermos has removable cup.

Pit-a-Pat wooden tray is decorated with scraps.

Hinged wooden step-ladder.

Metal drum filled with sand.

Red fire bucket contains water.

GAS MASK, RATION BOOKS, AND IDENTITY CARD *(RIGHT)* The gas mask, of paper, talc, and tape, is a genuine wartime model. The two ration books and the blue identity card are later replicas of originals, now missing from the house.

Replica miniature ration book.

Miniature gas mask made from paper and talc.

MALE DOLL *(BELOW)*
It was beyond the owner's skill to copy her father's army uniform, so the male doll became an air raid warden instead. The suit, collar, and tie were his original outfit, but the "ARP" (Air Raid Protection) arm-band and helmet were homemade.

Protective tin hat made by dolls' house owner.

Heavy metal shovel from antique set.

Painted ceramic doll with jointed shoulders and hips.

Original, commercially made blue felt dolls' suit.

Flat feet, with painted shoes, enable doll to stand unaided.

Sand used to deal with incendiary bombs.

MODERN HOUSE

—— English; designed and made by Christopher Cole in the 1970s ——

ALTHOUGH BOTH CRAFTSMEN and commercial firms have produced a great deal of excellent new miniature furniture, often replicas of contemporary pieces, very few dolls' houses have been made in designs that reflect modern architecture. This extremely unusual 1970s example was an early design by Christopher Cole, a doctor who began making dolls' houses partly because of his interest in architecture, and partly because he wished to have a hobby that he could develop into a full-time occupation when he retired.

The house, which was sold as a kit, is constructed of lightly varnished birch plywood, with a long side window panel and front door made of clear plastic. It has removable floors, and pegged interior walls and stairs, designed to allow children to create differently shaped rooms within a firm basic structure, thus stimulating imaginative play. Children proved to be more conventional than anticipated, however, preferring traditional-looking dolls' houses, so Christopher Cole altered his plans and relatively few houses like this were ever produced.

Window panels incorporated into basic structural design.

Floors planned to be seen through window panels.

Entrance hall has plastic, plate-glass-effect door and panel.

Floor supported by strips of wood on interior side walls.

On second and third floors, stairs peg into holes on left side interior walls.

Red dye-cast metal 1949-style "Coccinelle Berline" Volkswagen, made by French firm Solido.

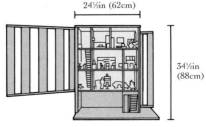

24½in (62cm)

34½in (88cm)

Wood and plastic; hinged facade and side panel.

THE FACADE
Clear plastic strips between wooden panels, crossed by the horizontal lines of the floors, form a striking facade on this representation of a modern four-story building. The area below the house is left open, for use as a shop or carport, as the owner wishes.

Painted metal bicycle with rubber wheels, made in China c.1950.

Open front area, used here as carport.

Opening side window extends from roof to ground level.

External and internal walls are of plain varnished plywood.

Inner walls peg into holes in floors.

Plastic and metal chair by Brio.

Floor designed to slide out of framework.

Television, bookcase, and record player by Lundby.

Stairs from first floor emerge on landing.

Pegs on right side wall hold first flight of stairs.

Black plastic strip on door provides handle.

Base wider on right side to accommodate opening side panel.

Firm base provides essential support for this type of house.

FOURTH FLOOR

The bathroom *(center)*, with hinged doors to the rooms on either side, is fitted with Lundby units, while the main bedroom *(right)* contains a selection of wood and plastic pieces. The landing on the left is furnished as a teenager's "pad" with furniture made by Hansi.

THIRD FLOOR

The interior walls have been moved to provide a large dining room between the landing *(left)* and the small kitchen *(right)*. The Scandinavian furniture is mainly plastic, with some wooden items in the kitchen, including a kitchen unit by the Danish firm Hansi; the wood-effect shelving unit in the dining room is by Brio.

SECOND FLOOR

There is only one room on this floor as the stairs, oddly, switch from the right side to the left, creating a landing on either side of the living room. The internal walls have archways connecting the landings and living room, which is filled with furniture made by Brio.

FIRST FLOOR

The entrance hall *(right)* has a clear plastic plate-glass-effect front panel and a hinged door. A Volkswagen Beetle is parked in the open space, along with a bicycle and two garbage cans.

SCANDINAVIAN STYLE

THE FURNITURE in Christopher Cole's 1970s-style house was chosen to represent the type of contemporary designs that a busy professional family might have chosen during that period. Most of the pieces are Scandinavian, made by the Swedish firms Lundby and Brio and by the Danish firm Hansi. Hansi products were mostly made of wood, with some fabric. Lundby, too, produced wooden furniture, but, like Brio, it also made some excellent miniature replicas of modern items, using molded plastics.

Daisies in plastic vase.

Molded plastic and metal chair.

Wooden tea set is German.

Miniature replica plastic coffeemaker.

English-made wooden table.

TABLE AND CHAIR (ABOVE)

On the plain wooden table are a realistic miniature replica coffeemaker and plastic vase of flowers by Lundby; the plastic and metal chair was made by Brio.

Miniature replica of contemporary furniture, made by Brio.

Red-flocked armchair swivels on metal base.

Goblet, vase, and plastic table with flocked top all by Lundby.

Contemporary use of metal in furniture reflected by Brio miniatures.

Detailed realistic toothbrushes, toothbrush holders, and soap.

SOFA AND CHAIR

(LEFT) In the 1970s and 80s, influenced by the designer Arne Jacobsen, Brio made some replicas of modern furniture. The red sofa and armchair are two famous examples.

BATHROOM UNITS (BELOW/RIGHT)

Lundby has produced dolls' house furniture and miniatures since the 1950s. These units and realistic, well-designed accessories, illustrate the company's attention to detail.

Realistic shower stall is part of bathroom set.

Bath unit has integral tiled wall section.

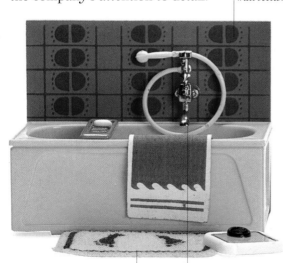

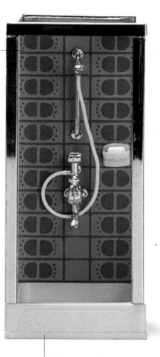

Bathroom set includes bath-mats, scale, and soap rack.

Bath has hand-held shower, and other accessories.

Shower unit matches bath in coordinated bathroom set.

"His and hers" basins in bathroom unit.

Plastic "electric" razor plugged into socket.

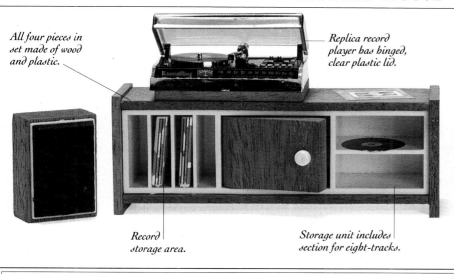

All four pieces in set made of wood and plastic.

Replica record player has hinged, clear plastic lid.

Miniature "stereophonic" loudspeaker.

Record storage area.

Storage unit includes section for eight-tracks.

RECORD PLAYER AND STORAGE UNIT (*LEFT*)
The meticulous attention to detail makes these items highly realistic. Many of the parts are movable; for example, the arm of the authentic-looking record player can be moved from rest to play position.

Molded plastic gives mesh effect at front of loudspeaker.

A TYPICAL 1970s FAMILY

THE DOLLS' HOUSE OWNER, who intended to record contemporary fashions as well as furnishing trends, commissioned these dolls from Barbara Cox, who designed and made them with flexible bodies and limbs, embroidered stockinette-covered faces, and wool hair. After consultations about the dolls' characters, they were then dressed appropriately. The family consists of a father, visualized as a television producer, the mother (an author), her retired father, a teenage son, two young children (boy and girl twins), and a baby; an au pair is also included in the household. Only four members of the family are shown here – father, mother, teenage son, and the au pair.

Father wears fashionable turtleneck sweater and suede jacket and trousers.

Only jacket is removable.

Au pair knits with yellow wool on steel pins.

Teenage son wears "flower-power" shirt and flared jeans.

Wool hair and embroidered features.

Mother wears suede jacket and velvet pant-suit.

Flexible dolls can hold any chosen position.

Au pair wears high boots and miniskirt.

Blue version of Brio chairs.

PLAYMOBIL HOUSE

German; first produced by Geobra Brandstätter in 1989

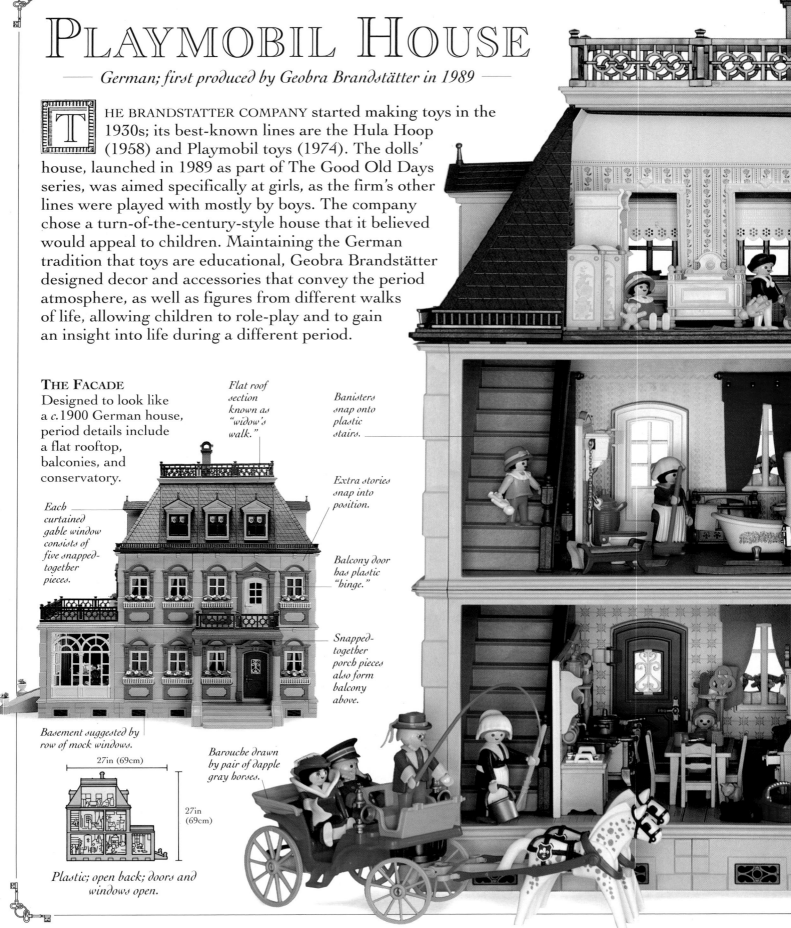

THE BRANDSTATTER COMPANY started making toys in the 1930s; its best-known lines are the Hula Hoop (1958) and Playmobil toys (1974). The dolls' house, launched in 1989 as part of The Good Old Days series, was aimed specifically at girls, as the firm's other lines were played with mostly by boys. The company chose a turn-of-the-century-style house that it believed would appeal to children. Maintaining the German tradition that toys are educational, Geobra Brandstätter designed decor and accessories that convey the period atmosphere, as well as figures from different walks of life, allowing children to role-play and to gain an insight into life during a different period.

THE FACADE
Designed to look like a *c.*1900 German house, period details include a flat rooftop, balconies, and conservatory.

Flat roof section known as "widow's walk."

Banisters snap onto plastic stairs.

Each curtained gable window consists of five snapped-together pieces.

Extra stories snap into position.

Balcony door has plastic "hinge."

Snapped-together porch pieces also form balcony above.

Basement suggested by row of mock windows.

Barouche drawn by pair of dapple gray horses.

27in (69cm)

27in (69cm)

Plastic; open back; doors and windows open.

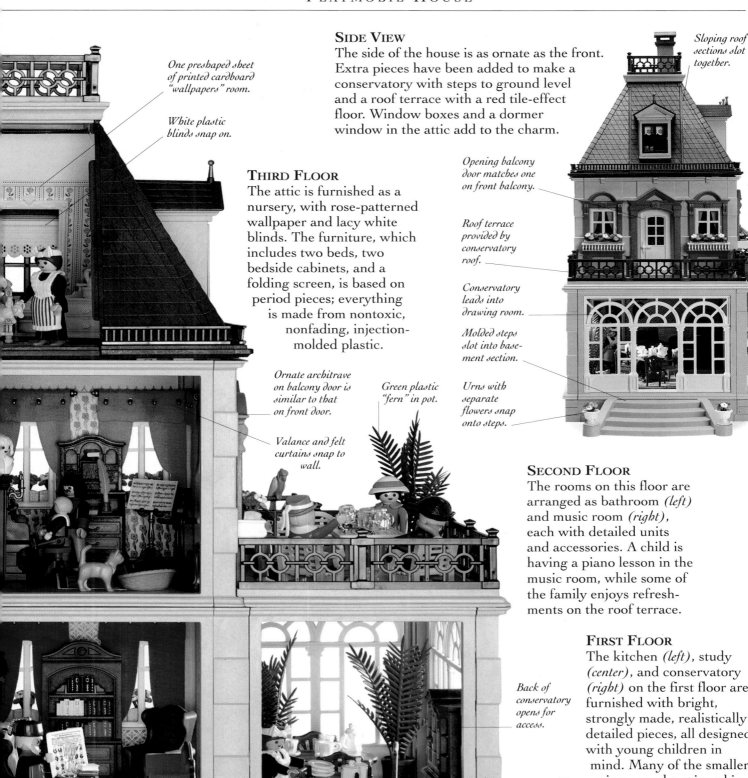

One preshaped sheet of printed cardboard "wallpapers" room.

White plastic blinds snap on.

SIDE VIEW
The side of the house is as ornate as the front. Extra pieces have been added to make a conservatory with steps to ground level and a roof terrace with a red tile-effect floor. Window boxes and a dormer window in the attic add to the charm.

Sloping roof sections slot together.

THIRD FLOOR
The attic is furnished as a nursery, with rose-patterned wallpaper and lacy white blinds. The furniture, which includes two beds, two bedside cabinets, and a folding screen, is based on period pieces; everything is made from nontoxic, nonfading, injection-molded plastic.

Opening balcony door matches one on front balcony.

Roof terrace provided by conservatory roof.

Conservatory leads into drawing room.

Molded steps slot into basement section.

Ornate architrave on balcony door is similar to that on front door.

Green plastic "fern" in pot.

Urns with separate flowers snap onto steps.

Valance and felt curtains snap to wall.

SECOND FLOOR
The rooms on this floor are arranged as bathroom (left) and music room (right), each with detailed units and accessories. A child is having a piano lesson in the music room, while some of the family enjoys refreshments on the roof terrace.

FIRST FLOOR
The kitchen (left), study (center), and conservatory (right) on the first floor are furnished with bright, strongly made, realistically detailed pieces, all designed with young children in mind. Many of the smaller pieces can be gripped in the dolls' viselike hands where appropriate.

Back of conservatory opens for access.

Baby carriage has movable wheels — and occupant.

playmobil 1900

PLASTIC FURNISHINGS

MOST PLAYMOBIL FURNITURE is sold in room-set packs with accessories included. Items from the bathroom, kitchen, and music room sets are featured here. Some pieces, like the piano, are freestanding, while others are attached to walls. Almost all the items are made of injection-molded plastic, but there are also some fabric accessories, such as felt curtains with valances, bathroom towels, and printed composition rugs.

Playmobil head incorporated into luminous bust.

"Gilt" candle in sconce.

MUSIC SET (BELOW)
The piano plays *Für Elise* when the keys are pressed. The set includes a music stand and music teacher.

Miniature Beethoven score.

Revolving red seat on piano stool.

"Schimmel" piano with hinged lid.

Movable chain on tank.

Toilet has hinged lid.

Printed paper mat around base of toilet.

Gilt lamp and mirror above basin.

BATHROOM UNITS (ABOVE)
Both bathroom units shown here are designed to provide extra walls if required. The toilet seat and chain are both movable, and the set includes printed paper mats, a bath, stove, and towel rail.

KITCHEN UNITS (BELOW)
Both units are attached to wall plates and have movable accessories, such as the mugs and plates in the shelves by the sink. Two "copper" pans sit on the stove, above which is a rack of kitchen utensils.

Utensils include rolling pin and meat mallet.

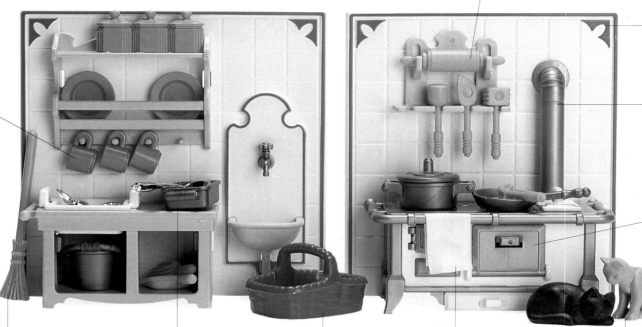

Orange mug hangs from shelf unit.

Back plate provides extra wall if necessary.

Pipe runs from stove to back wall plate.

Door of kitchen stove opens.

Yellow plastic broom is part of kitchen set.

Tray of "silver" cutlery on drainboard.

Kitchen basket made of molded plastic.

White fabric towel hanging on rail.

Gray cat has movable head.

PLAYMOBIL FAMILY AND STAFF

PLAYMOBIL DOLLS are designed to be safe and easy for young children to hold, attractively colorful, and free of sharp edges. They have no mechanical parts, but the heads are movable and the dolls can stand, sit, and hold objects in their viselike hands, allowing children to develop and use their imagination to the fullest as they play. The injection-molded plastic dolls were designed by Hans Beck, who was influenced by children's drawings of people. As it is company policy that all the dolls' faces must look alike, Beck developed a pattern suitable for all the characters portrayed, using simple round heads with dots for eyes and a curve for the mouth. The facial features are molded, not painted on, so they will not rub off.

THE STAFF *(RIGHT)* The costumes worn by the coachman and the three maids are more colorful than strictly accurate for 1900, but their design does successfully suggest the period.

EXTENDED FAMILY *(BELOW)* All three generations have the same Playmobil body design; the children are simply smaller versions, first introduced in 1981 by Geobra Brandstätter.

Bearded coachman wears spectacles and blue hat.

Housemaid's cap is removable.

Parlor maid in afternoon uniform.

Tea cart, laden with "china," has moving wheels.

Coachman wears breeches and red knee-high boots.

Second housemaid wears morning uniform.

Hands swivel at wrists to grasp tea cart.

Musician holds removable quill pen.

Arms jointed at shoulders.

Grandfather wears removable blue cap.

Small boy wears green neckerchief.

Family parrot can be removed from perch.

Logo can be seen on base of little girl's foot.

Design allows doll to bend at waist.

playmobil® 1900

UNUSUAL DOLLS' HOUSES

There seems to be no limit to the creativity of dolls' house makers. Not only can they produce realistic and fantastic miniature buildings for individually commissioned projects, but their choice of material varies from wood and paper to Popsicle sticks and split bamboo — and includes marzipan and ice for exhibition pieces. The examples featured in this book come from many countries: they are both antique and modern, collectors' items and playthings.

DOLLS' HOUSE DESIGNERS, particularly those artist-craftsmen and -women who make one house for a specially commissioned order or to indulge their own personal creativity, do seem sometimes to have looked at full-scale houses and thought "anything you can do I can do better." For, unrestricted by any practical demands of reality, their choice of building materials alone is ingenious: paper, matchsticks, glass, and tubular steel — such examples are almost commonplace, even for constructions that are destined to become the antiques and collectors' items of the future.

As for those ephemeral creations required only for the duration of an exhibition, two particularly memorable personal favorites are a replica of a Christian Hacker butcher's shop, made entirely of colored marzipan, and an exquisite, sparkling ice nativity scene, which was flown from Canada to Paris for a Christmas exhibition, where it was displayed in a glass-fronted refrigerator.

— RARE EXAMPLES —

To be classified as unusual, though, a dolls' house or room setting does not have to be made of exotic materials; it is the maker's imagination, or the rarity of the piece, that makes such a description apt or accurate. To most European or American collectors, any dolls' house resembling a Japanese home would be regarded as an unusual prize for their collection. Although the delicacy of Japanese models makes them collectors' items in many countries, and they are not often found outside Japan, they are by no means unique objets d'art. The dolls' house featured on pp.120–23 is extremely unusual, however, as an

JAPANESE MINIATURE HOUSE *(LEFT)*
This exquisitely made house, just 7½in (19cm) high, probably dates from c.1900. Woven bamboo panels form the roof and foundations, and the perfectly made wall panels slide along grooves at the top and bottom.

CANADIAN DOLLS' HOUSE *(RIGHT)*
Made in Canada in the 1870s, this glass-doored cabinet house has a curving staircase connecting the two rooms and an unusual, inaccessible attic, which is lit by stained-glass inserts in the gable and by windows in the roof. The attic contains paper-scrap figures and artificial flowers.

example of this size, and one made as a child's plaything, is rare even in Japan, the country where it was bought. For centuries, Japanese children have had a fine variety of toys and dolls to play with as well as to admire; but the miniature palaces, temples, houses, or pieces of lacquered furniture that were popular in Japanese homes, were intended for display purposes only – a dolls' house as a plaything was never a traditional Japanese toy.

Another rare dolls' house made in Southeast Asia is the Tibetan example on pp.124–27, which is thought to be the only one of its kind in Europe. Like the Japanese dolls' house, it fascinates Western eyes by presenting a totally different style of architecture and interior

decoration. The Tibetan house was constructed relatively recently, in the 1980s; a much earlier and cruder wooden dolls' house than this is a rare example from Russia, which is now on display in the Precinct Toy Museum in Sandwich, Kent, England. It is only about 18in (46cm) high and, like the box on which it stands, it is handpainted in traditional red and green decoration. All that is known of its history is that it came from Kirov, in Siberia, and was probably brought to England during the Russian Revolution.

Often, part of the charm of unusual dolls' houses is their capacity to stimulate interest in, and often to evoke memories of, a past way of life in far-off lands. The Guyanese dolls' house *(see pp.128–29)* was made by a woman who now lives in London but still remembers her family home in Guyana, which she has simplified but otherwise

BUILDING BLOCKS *(LEFT)* In the nineteenth century a German printer, Richter of Rudolstadt, produced boxed sets of building blocks. This illustration is from a booklet advertising the complete line.

MATCHBOX ROOM *(RIGHT)*
This minuscule sickroom is one of a very popular German series of rooms and scenes in matchboxes. The series, which is still in production, includes rural and nativity scenes, kitchens, and schoolrooms, all with tiny wooden figures in printed settings.

DOLLS' HOUSE CAROUSEL *(LEFT)*
A modern example of an old favorite — a pop-up book that provides a two-story, eight-room dolls' house, complete with a fold-up staircase and opening doors and cupboards.

MINIATURE "BLISS" DOLLS' HOUSE *(RIGHT)*
Made in the United States, this modern paper version of a Bliss-type dolls' house has external features printed on. The open back reveals two rooms.

faithfully reproduced in miniature as a child's plaything. A completely different use of natural unpainted wood is demonstrated by architectural student Jane Blyth with her imaginative creation, the Weavers' House *(see pp.116–17)*. Jane described the necessary materials for her most unusual structures as being "space, light, and shade;" wood seems almost to be an afterthought.

— HISTORICAL DIMENSIONS —

Wood was all-important, though, to Henry Hall, the master mariner who built and furnished Contented Cot *(see pp.114–115)* for his baby daughter in 1886. To have such a special dolls' house must have delighted the child later on; her father pasted the newspaper announcement of her birth over the attic window and carved his initials on some of the furniture. Unfortunately, we do not know if Contented Cot is a miniature version of the Halls' own cottage.

However, there is another

dolls' house currently under construction that is an exact replica of a real London home. It has features such as stained-glass windows, metal "cast-iron" balusters, plaster moldings, cornices, and friezes, as well as external ironwork and balustrades, all created as exact 1:12 replicas of the originals *(see p.134)*. The miniature house is intended to be a record of a family home during three generations' occupancy, providing a very unusual three-dimensional "document."

Unusual dolls' houses on a grand scale include magnificent buildings such as the Queen Mary's Dolls' House, in Windsor Castle, England, and Titania's Palace, in Legoland, Denmark. The Fairy Castle of Colleen Moore, which is displayed in Chicago's Museum of Science and Industry, is a wonderful fantasy, realized by the best of Hollywood's artists and imaginative craftsmen.

The revival of interest in miniature houses, which have been designed and built for adults to decorate and furnish with beautiful artifacts, has resulted in a number of unique houses being created for today's collectors — particularly those in the United Kingdom and the United States.

Some English stately homes that do not have an heirloom miniature house to display are showing wonderful modern examples that have been

JAPANESE NESTING HOUSES *(LEFT) These five small boxlike houses, of stained and printed wood, fit into each other like the better-known Russian matryoshka dolls.*

created and furnished by highly skilled artist-craftsmen. Two such makers of miniature buildings with especially fine interior decoration and furniture are John Hodgson and Kevin Mulvaney. John Hodgson has produced a series of period residences for display at Hever Castle, Edenbridge, Kent, England, while two of Kevin Mulvaney's creations have traveled far and wide: Britannia House tours to raise funds for the African Medical Research Foundation, and another model, based on a wing of Versailles, was bought by the Californian Angels' Attic Museum. It is also used to raise funds for charity.

— DOLLS' HOUSE OCCUPANTS —

Sometimes beautiful buildings have very unusual occupants. Colleen Moore's Castle and Titania's Palace were designed for invisible elves and fairies, while Mirror Grange was a home built for Pip, Squeak, and Wilfred – a dog, penguin, and rabbit who appeared daily in a cartoon in a British newspaper during the 1920s and 30s. This fascinating "house on a rock," which was designed by Maxwell Ayrton, also raised funds for charity.

Coming down to earth, or rather to the level of the nursery floor, unusual dwellings for dolls have often been popular toys. During the 1920s and 1930s, some interesting wooden "mobile homes" were produced, including trailers and even a houseboat on invisible wheels (see pp.118–19). Two modern equivalents of these are now available: Mattel's Barbie

doll has an ingeniously designed mobile home, while the Sylvanian animals inhabit a canal boat. Both of these toys are plastic.

Children and adults have always been fascinated by tiny things. At the turn of the century "The Smallest" series of rooms in a matchbox was produced (see p.111); today, plastic versions are advertised as "pocket-sized playmates." Of course, dolls' house nurseries must have their own dolls' houses and a number of these are available, ranging from plastic models and reproduction Bliss-type printed cardboard designs to limited editions made from thin painted wood.

It really goes without saying that, for the makers of dolls' houses that can be grouped into a category named "unusual," the range and scope is almost unlimited. They certainly seem to have used every possible – and sometimes seemingly impossible – material when constructing them.

BARBIE'S MOBILE HOME
(BELOW) The ingenious design of Barbie's mobile home allows the vehicle to open into two sections; it provides Barbie with a fully furnished studio on wheels, decorated in pink, white, and gold.

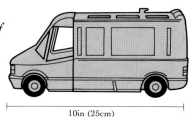

10in (25cm)

ATTIC STUDIO
Part of the back roof, with a skylight, is hinged, revealing the artist at work in his studio. A newspaper clipping pasted above the dormer window announces the birth of Henry Hall's daughter in 1886.

Metal bar across front of high chair is removable.

Artist doll, dressed in smock and floppy hat, works at painting on easel.

Slate tile-effect horizontal roof sections fit together when closed.

Sand shaken over newly painted walls gives stucco effect.

Wallpapers, carpet, and curtain materials all date from c.1880s.

Carved wooden mantelpiece with small metal fender.

China-headed doll with bisque limbs and soft body.

Dining chair, made by Henry Hall as part of dining room set.

Grooves in floor and ceiling allow back wall section to slide out.

Henry Hall's initials carved on piano.

Painted, carved wood and wire light fixture.

Mirror in gilded frame hangs above mantelpiece.

PIANO AND CHAIRS
(ABOVE) The furniture is simply and sturdily made, but Henry Hall's artistic skill is revealed by his use of gilt decoration and the piano's fretwork motif. The balloon-backed high chair matches the dining chairs.

Dining room carpet made from Victorian petit-point bag.

CONTENTED COT

—— English; made by Devonshire sea captain in 1886 ——

WITH ITS NAME, DATE, MAKER, and first owner all recorded in or on its structure, this is one of the few dolls' houses with a known provenance. Along with the name above the door and the date over the attic window, a newspaper clipping announcing the "Birth ... October 11th at Mount Pleasant Road, Brixham (Devon), wife of Henry Hall, Master Mariner, of a daughter" is pasted inside the attic. Unfortunately, the first name of the daughter, for whom the house was made, is unknown. Much of the original furniture remains, some marked "H.H."; other pieces of furniture and dolls have been added, all of the same period and scale. The present owner hopes that research will reveal if the dolls' house resembles the Brixham home of Henry Hall, the house's talented creator.

Small wooden sash window glides smoothly up and down in frame.

China-headed maid, with bisque limbs and soft body, wears original morning uniform.

SECOND FLOOR
The upper room is furnished as a sitting room with a simple wooden bed plus a carved chaise longue and an upholstered settee. A door behind the fixed wall leads to the stairs.

House name carved above door.

Lever outside front door activates bell in attic.

Back door sealed; all other doors and windows (except attic skylight) will open.

Chimney serves two fire-places below.

Front roof does not move.

Hinged double casement windows open inward.

Panels of perforated tin attached to wooden rail form balcony.

Extended base forms walkway around house.

Seashells decorate base.

FIRST FLOOR
The first floor comprises a dining room, hall, and stairs, visible only through the opened front door. A section of the back wall, with painted back door, does not move; the other section slides out to give access.

THE FACADE
"Contented Cot" is carved in a curve over the front door, complementing the window arches. The wood-and-metal balcony, carved finials, ridgepole, and gabled attic window illustrate the maker's skill and artistry; the sand-covered walls and seashell ornamentation are clues to his maritime past.

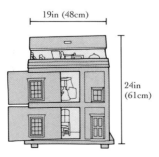

19in (48cm)

24in (61cm)

Two sliding panels in back; rear roof section hinged.

WEAVERS' HOUSE

— English; designed and made by Jane Blyth; c.1970 —

T HIS HOUSE IS A PARADOX: designed as a child's toy, it also intrigues adults. It is a modern structure, solid enough for active play, but capable of changing shape. Perhaps a clue lies in the words of its creator, who expects it to be "taken to pieces without falling apart." Jane Blyth wanted the house to be a toy that would stimulate creative play and that children would enjoy.

The house has a conventionally shaped roof, but otherwise its construction depends on the imagination of the owner. Although the house can be formed into complex patterns, it is made from simple and easily found materials – Popsicle sticks, doweling, string, pieces of linen, clothespins, etc. Since making her first house, Jane Blyth has created several other "theme" houses and entered a multicultural nativity scene/house in *Architectural Design* magazine's competition of 1983.

Wood, though smooth, is unpainted and unpolished.

Ladder can double as fence.

Hanks of string hang from peg, ready for weaving.

Lengths of wood interlink to form pitched roof.

Window shutters slide across horizontal planks.

BASIC STRUCTURE (*LEFT*)
According to Jane Blyth, her houses "are made of wood, light, shadows, and spaces." The house shape can vary with the owner's whim, since many of the lengths of plain timber are interchangeable: attics can have windows or shutters, slatted base sections can be altered, and only the side uprights are fixed. All connections, apart from one wood joint, are made with pegs and holes.

Hank of string forms hair.

Wooden clothespin doll with eyes only facial feature.

Symbolic "heart of house" hangs on side wall.

Deck shape can change, depending on number of sections used.

Simple wooden tub with handle.

14in (36cm)

18in (46cm)

Side uprights do not move; everything else can be moved.

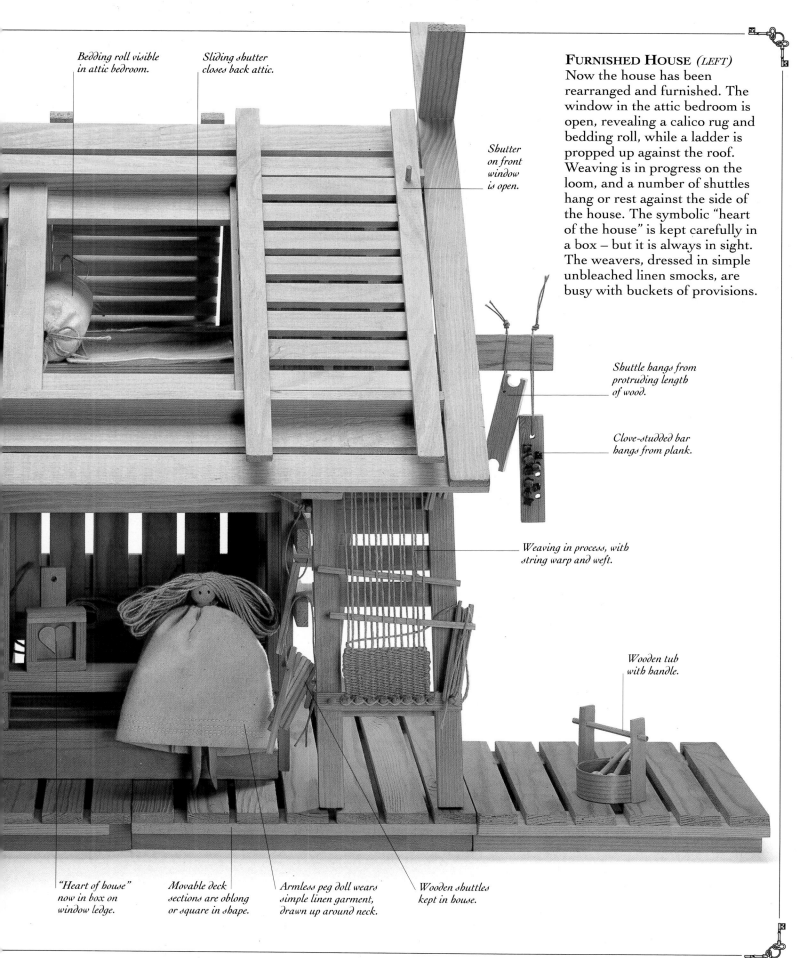

Bedding roll visible
in attic bedroom.

Sliding shutter
closes back attic.

Shutter
on front
window
is open.

FURNISHED HOUSE *(LEFT)*
Now the house has been
rearranged and furnished. The
window in the attic bedroom is
open, revealing a calico rug and
bedding roll, while a ladder is
propped up against the roof.
Weaving is in progress on the
loom, and a number of shuttles
hang or rest against the side of
the house. The symbolic "heart
of the house" is kept carefully in
a box – but it is always in sight.
The weavers, dressed in simple
unbleached linen smocks, are
busy with buckets of provisions.

Shuttle hangs from
protruding length
of wood.

Clove-studded bar
hangs from plank.

Weaving in process, with
string warp and weft.

Wooden tub
with handle.

"Heart of house"
now in box on
window ledge.

Movable deck
sections are oblong
or square in shape.

Armless peg doll wears
simple linen garment,
drawn up around neck.

Wooden shuttles
kept in house.

MOBILE HOMES

— German trailer and English houseboat; early 20th century —

THESE UNUSUAL PAINTED mobile homes for dolls were designed as children's playthings. Both are sturdily constructed and offer scope for imaginative play, in addition to their basic attraction as pull toys.

The trailer, which has a decorative stenciled pattern on the external walls, is of a more complex design than the houseboat; the porch at one end is adorned with flower boxes, and a drawer beneath the main section provides storage for the wooden porch steps when the trailer is on the move.

The chief ornamentation on the houseboat is the splendid railed deck – albeit with a practical stove pipe pushing through. A rugged, carved wooden Captain stands on deck, contrasting vividly with the two daintily dressed, jointed bisque French dolls who occupy the trailer. The solid metal wheels underneath the houseboat are hidden.

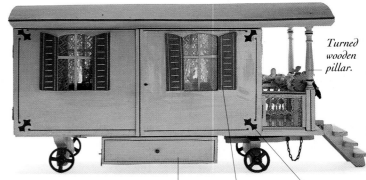

Turned wooden pillar.

THE FACADE

This enchanting trailer has a pair of green painted wooden shutters at each lace-curtained window; the porch, with its gilded metal balustrade, is supported by wooden pillars.

Drawer for stowing steps when not in use.

Painted wooden "louvered" shutter attached to wall.

Simple blue pattern on doors.

THE TRAILER

It seems that no child had the joy of playing with this charming toy: the wallpapers are unmarked, the net curtains and shining "brass" cornices are immaculate, and the furniture is just as it left the factory – still tied through the painted cardboard floor covering. White and gold embossed paper decorates the furniture in the French style.

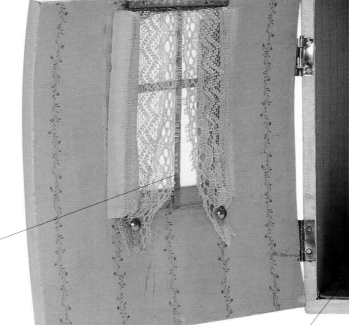

Painted paper mullions stuck to window glass.

Dark blue printed paper "upholstery."

Spoked metal wheel on strong wooden axle.

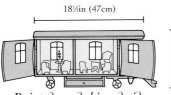

18½in (47cm)

10in (25cm)

Painted wood; hinged side openings and porch door.

WASHINGTON DOLLS' HOUSE & TOY MUSEUM

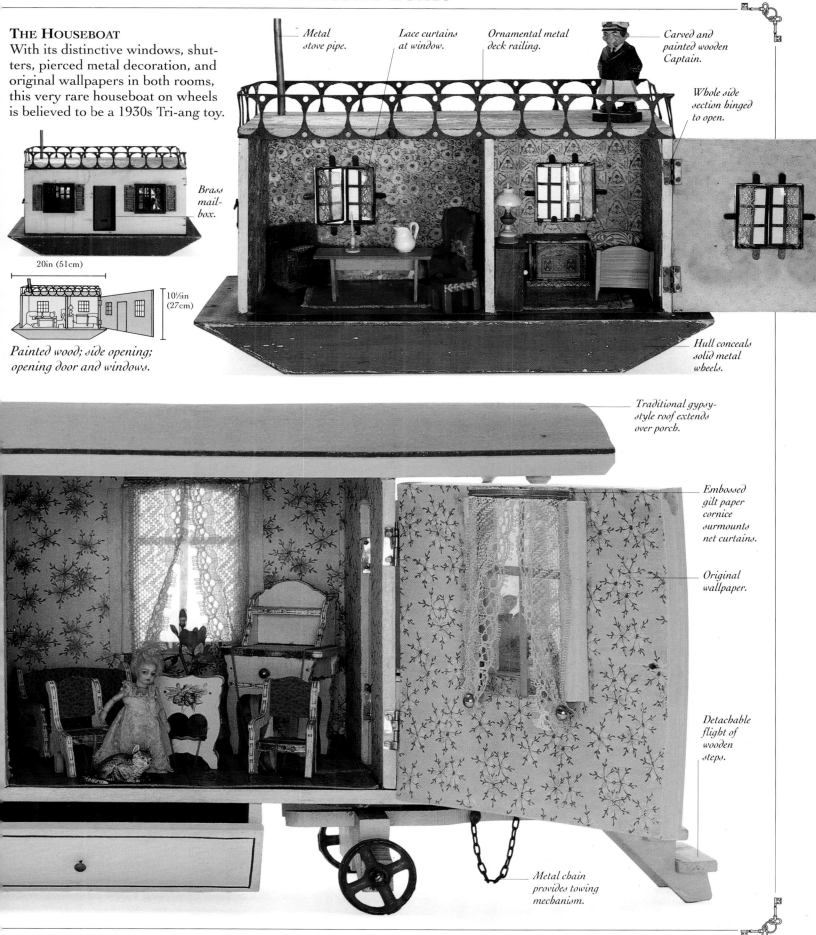

THE HOUSEBOAT
With its distinctive windows, shutters, pierced metal decoration, and original wallpapers in both rooms, this very rare houseboat on wheels is believed to be a 1930s Tri-ang toy.

20in (51cm)

10½in (27cm)

Painted wood; side opening; opening door and windows.

Metal stove pipe.

Lace curtains at window.

Ornamental metal deck railing.

Carved and painted wooden Captain.

Whole side section hinged to open.

Brass mail-box.

Hull conceals solid metal wheels.

Traditional gypsy-style roof extends over porch.

Embossed gilt paper cornice surmounts net curtains.

Original wallpaper.

Detachable flight of wooden steps.

Metal chain provides towing mechanism.

JAPANESE HOUSE

— Japanese dolls' house; shipped to England in 1952 —

A DOLLS' HOUSE such as this is rare, even in Japan, and it is possible that this was made as a special commission. It is known only that an English photographer who visited Japan in 1952 brought the dolls' house back as a present for his young daughter. Although the house is designed as a dolls' house, it is also an authentic replica of a nineteenth-century Japanese dwelling, with its sliding wooden screens, external bath house, and simple room furnishings. Rooms in Japanese houses are measured by the number of mats needed to cover the floors; for example, the upper rooms in this house are six-mat size, while the lower room is eight-mat size. Like the mats, the interior and exterior screens are perfect replicas and slide along grooves in the floors and ceilings.

Rolled-up futon.

Paper sunshade.

SECOND FLOOR
The room on the left has a closet with sliding slatted screens, behind which futons are stored. The other room, with a shrine in the alcove, is an important guest room; such a room is found in all traditional Japanese homes.

Bath house, entered from house or by external entrance, contains wooden bathtub and toilet.

Hinged door to bath house.

Closet for storing external screens when not in use.

Projecting porch protects main entrance to house.

THE FACADE
This house, of natural wood, has no glazed windows; ventilation, protection from the elements, and light are provided by screens. Heavier screens are kept in a closet on the veranda.

Kitchen, behind screen on platform, has sliding doors to living area.

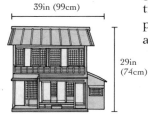

39in (99cm)

29in (74cm)

Natural wood; screens slide back or can be removed.

FIRST FLOOR
Silver-papered wooden screens divide the house's largest room from the staircase, vestibule, and external bath house *(right)*. Similar screens divide the kitchen from the living area.

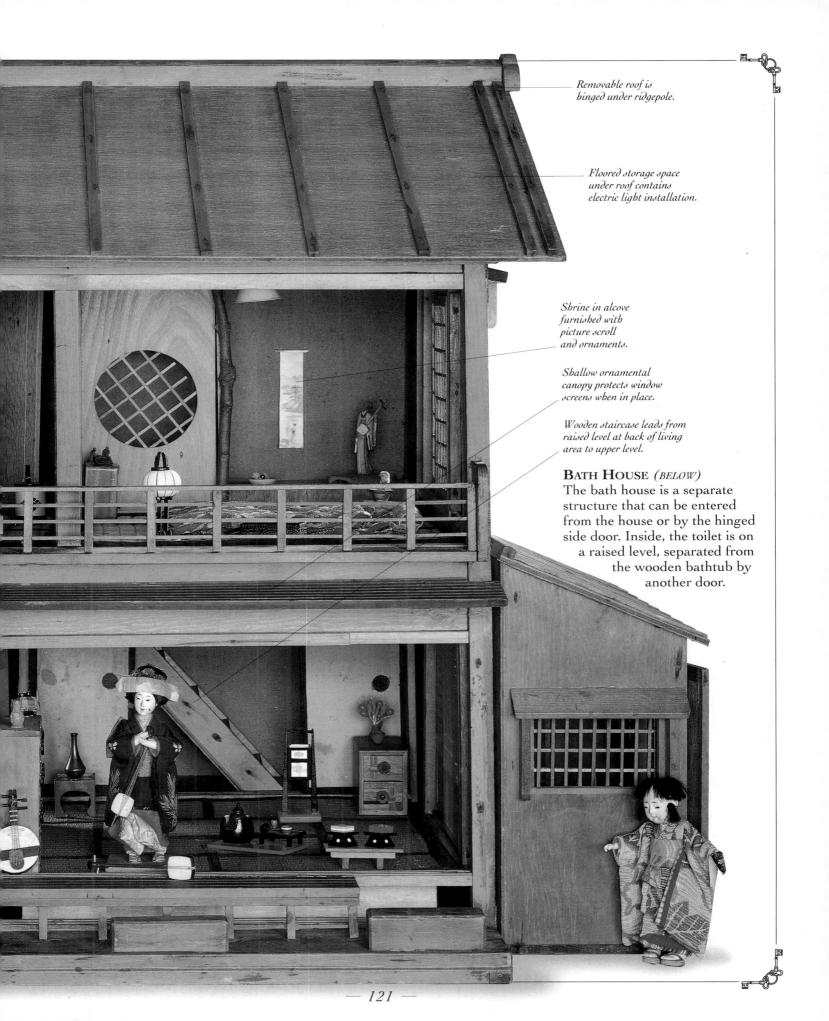

Removable roof is hinged under ridgepole.

Floored storage space under roof contains electric light installation.

Shrine in alcove furnished with picture scroll and ornaments.

Shallow ornamental canopy protects window screens when in place.

Wooden staircase leads from raised level at back of living area to upper level.

BATH HOUSE *(BELOW)*
The bath house is a separate structure that can be entered from the house or by the hinged side door. Inside, the toilet is on a raised level, separated from the wooden bathtub by another door.

JAPANESE STYLE

JAPANESE FURNISHINGS are often stored when not in use, leaving rooms uncluttered. Using futons instead of beds, for example, means that sleeping areas are quickly converted into living rooms. Paper lanterns light the rooms and a few carefully selected ornaments, flowers, and paintings are displayed. The sparse ornamentation and plain walls contribute to the serene effect of Japanese homes. Black or red lacquered items decorated with gold, such as the two small boxes shown here, are particularly prized possessions.

SIX-MAT ROOM (*RIGHT*)
In Japan, straw and string mats bound with black linen are always laid in a traditional pattern. Placed on the mats are three antique stringed instruments, two tiny black lacquered boxes (for writing equipment and a fan), a lamp on a red lacquered base, and a blue-covered bedding roll (futon); the two low tables hold food and ornaments.

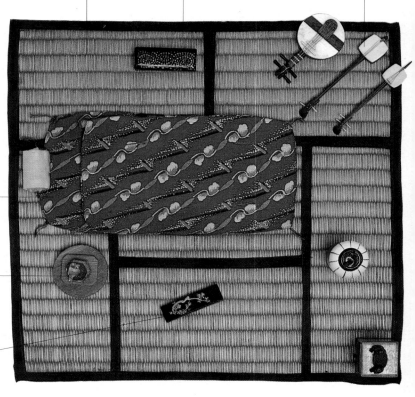

Floor mats made of string and straw.

Each mat bound with black linen.

Samisen – long, three-stringed Japanese instrument played with plectrum.

Bedding roll and pillow are stored in closet when not in use.

Flower arrangement placed on small table.

Black lacquered box with gold motif on lid.

KITCHEN (*LEFT*)
The cooking area is on the lower level, while the raised section provides storage space. The sink is piled high with vegetables, and on the green table are a wooden tray and bowls. The wooden mat is a practical floor covering.

Black lacquer lantern with paper shade.

Child enters kitchen from vestibule level.

Floor lantern set on red lacquer platform.

LANTERNS AND TEA SET
(*RIGHT/BELOW*) Candles or oil lamps light these decorative paper lanterns. Equipment for the ritual Japanese tea ceremony includes a fire pot and water dipper. The multicolored festival cakes, shown here on their special stands, are made for the Girls' Festival, which is held annually in March.

Festival cake.

Fire pot on red lacquer tray.

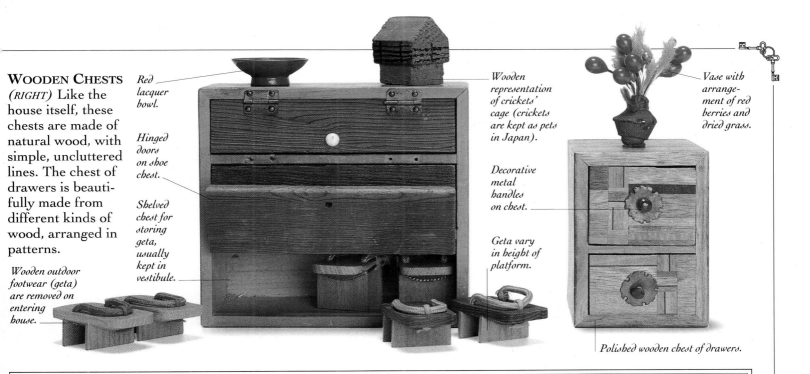

WOODEN CHESTS (RIGHT) Like the house itself, these chests are made of natural wood, with simple, uncluttered lines. The chest of drawers is beautifully made from different kinds of wood, arranged in patterns.

Red lacquer bowl.

Hinged doors on shoe chest.

Shelved chest for storing geta, usually kept in vestibule.

Wooden outdoor footwear (geta) are removed on entering house.

Wooden representation of crickets' cage (crickets are kept as pets in Japan).

Vase with arrangement of red berries and dried grass.

Decorative metal handles on chest.

Geta vary in height of platform.

Polished wooden chest of drawers.

ANTIQUE JAPANESE DOLLS

THESE ANTIQUE DOLLS, who have occupied the dolls' house since it arrived in England from Japan in 1952, came from a collection made by several generations of an English family that lived in Japan for many years. The dolls' heads are covered with a composition of pulverized oyster shells and glue, polished to resemble ivory, while their painted, molded hands fit onto the wired arms. The dolls, who are set in position on wooden stands, have tiny, inset glass eyes, and wigs, both simple and elaborate, that are correctly styled for each character. The intricately detailed costumes, worn by both men and women, include brocaded outer robes (kimonos), traditional sashes (obis), and padded silk undergarments.

Dolls' heads fit into padded wire foundations.

Little girl's kimono and obi are shorter than those of adults.

Elaborate ornamental combs hold hairstyles in place.

Sevenfold neckline of undergarments indicates high rank of wearer.

Traditional flower arrangement on stand.

Circular haircut and distinctive side-whiskers on young male doll.

Decorated paper scroll inscribed with poem.

Young boy doll holds modern hobby horse.

TIBETAN HOUSE

—— *Made in India by Lamaist monks in 1991* ——

THIS DOLLS' HOUSE is a representation of a traditional Tibetan house, made in India by monks from the Drepung Loseling monastery who were exiled with the Dalai Lama in 1959. In 1983, the monks resumed their traditional artistic skills and began making dolls and dolls' houses – partly to train new monks and partly to provide an income. This example is made of painted wood in the traditional Tibetan style, with gaily colored prayer flags flying from the two front corners. The monks blessed the house before packing and sending it off.

Female figure dressed in colorful Tibetan costume.

THE FACADE
The white facade, with brightly painted door and windows, is typical of a traditional Tibetan house. Each window has an external fabric blind, finished with a white pleated valance.

SECOND FLOOR
The Shrine Room *(right)* has an ornate, symbolically patterned ceiling, shrine, and wall hanging, while the room on the left contains a colorful prayer table and simple wooden bed.

Colorful prayer flags.

Incense jar fixed to balcony ledge.

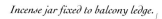

Window shade pulls out from window frame.

Each window has four glazed panes.

Base painted to represent bricks.

Hinged double doors painted red and green with large round ornamental handles.

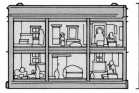

30in (76cm)

24in (61cm)

Wooden structure; back opening; hinged doors.

FIRST FLOOR
A large copper pot for storing grain dominates the kitchen *(left)*, while the middle room is furnished with a lacquered wooden sofabed. A carved male figure is seen at prayer in the room on the right.

Hinged door opens onto front balcony.

Internal window frame painted lighter shade of blue than exterior frame.

One of eight opening side windows.

Wooden beam ends painted to match exterior window frames.

Sliding door into entrance hall.

Walls painted pale green.

Power socket for house's lighting.

TIBETAN TRADITION

ALL THE FURNITURE made by the monks to furnish the Tibetan house is wooden; some pieces are painted but left unadorned, while others are profusely decorated with traditional Tibetan designs. The style of painting varies from the simple suggestion of lacquerwork on the sofabed in the middle room downstairs to the fine miniature painting of *Shakyamuni the Gotama* on the tanka in the Shrine Room. Other examples of Tibetan folk art decorate the shrine and prayer tables and the symbolically patterned ceiling in the Shrine Room. The sofa-bed upstairs is the only undecorated piece, apart from the contents of the kitchen, which include plain ceramic, wood, metal, and plaster items.

WALL HANGING

(*RIGHT*) This handpainted panel shows the deity Shakyamuni, founder of Indian Buddhism, *c*.500 BC. Surrounded by symbols, with the halo of enlighten-ment above his head, he sits in the lotus position. In his left hand is a monk's begging bowl; the right invokes the Earth's witness.

Shakyamuni represented with golden body and blue hair.

Black ceramic Tibetan mastiff.

Lhasa apso, in white ceramic.

TIBETAN DOGS (*LEFT*)

The dogs are painted ceramic. The larger, a Tibetan mastiff, is a watchdog, usually on guard outside the front door. The small dog is a Lhasa apso, a popular breed in Tibet long before it was seen in the West.

Deity sits on disk of sun and moon on lotus blossom.

Painting mounted on dark blue fabric backing.

Glazed cooking pot with removable lid.

Ornately decorated handpainted shrine.

Traditional Tibetan colors and patterns.

Long metal ladle with hooked handle.

Shell decoration on square black cooking stove.

Unglazed mixing bowl for kitchen use.

SHRINE AND SOFABED

(*LEFT/BELOW*) The shrine is painted in a popular Tibetan color scheme of red, yellow, and gold. A traditionally patterned mattress or bed board rests on the sofabed.

Imitation lacquer decoration.

COOKING EQUIPMENT

(*ABOVE*) The well-equipped kitchen has pots, pans, jars, and a set of unglazed pot-tery bowls. A large ceramic pot sits on the stove, which is fueled by dried yak's dung.

TIBETAN CHARACTERS

LIKE THE HOUSE and its contents, the dolls were carved by more than one craftsman, so each interpretation is unique, even though the proportions and characters for all the figures had been agreed upon. As scale was held to be of little importance, the dolls vary in size from 3–6in (8–15cm) in height. Even if the figures were individually carved, it appears that all the faces, and possibly the costumes, were painted by the same artist. There is certainly a family likeness, though each doll has a definite personal identity. Predictably, the monk's face is unlined and serene, unlike those of his two relatives who are praying with him.

PRAYING FIGURES *(BELOW)*

The monk of the family is joined by two relatives, each of whom holds a *mala* (Tibetan Buddhist rosary) and a prayer wheel.

Serene expression is well painted on realistic face.

Monk praying at decorated prayer table.

Prayer wheel, containing paper scroll, revolves to spin prayers.

Detailed facial expression with lines on forehead and face.

Tibetan Buddhist rosary of strung "pearl" beads.

Wooden hand pierced to hold prayer beads.

Monk sits on plain wooden bed board.

Multicolored apron is part of regional Tibetan costume.

Prayer table always placed by bed.

STANDING FIGURES *(BELOW)*

The dolls are beautifully carved and painted, with their colorful costumes designed to represent people from many regions of Tibet. The men wear colorful, traditional Tibetan padded boots.

Male doll wears traditional Tibetan cap.

Mother holds swaddled baby in arms.

Crown of hat is braided.

Regional variation of basic Tibetan man's costume.

Costume has decorative gold-painted pattern.

GUYANESE HOUSE

— Made by Guyanese student Ruth Bollers in 1992 —

RUTH BOLLERS, A GUYANESE student living in London, based this dolls' house on her childhood home, which she had recently revisited. Interested in craftwork, Ruth chose toymaking for her field of study at the London College of Furniture. She created this dolls' house as a toy, but was determined that it should accurately portray an aspect of Guyanese culture.

The house represents the type of dwelling found in Georgetown – the capital of Guyana – or in any similarly flat area of the country where flooding is frequent. Houses in such areas have structures of greenheart or purpleheart wood, with walls and floors of varnished pine or mahogany. Their furniture is usually made of pine, mahogany, cane, or a mixture of local woods whose coloring creates a toning effect.

The dolls' house contains essential items found in any Guyanese home – a hammock slung in the shade under the house, a mosquito net over the bed, and a rocking chair on the veranda, as well as a stove, tables, and chairs. Since Ruth made this house for my collection in 1992, I have added dolls and a basic shower and toilet, all made by Ruth to appropriate designs.

Wooden staircase provides access to front veranda.

Hinged door opens into room.

Verandas at front and rear of house provide extra living space.

Color-stained wooden chairs and settee.

Multi-colored woven rug with fringed ends.

Windows positioned to provide maximum ventilation.

Kitchen sink and stove of natural wood with silver-painted details.

Nontoxic wood dyes were used to color furniture.

OVERHEAD VIEW
The simple wooden furniture in the house was designed for young children.

Staircase gives access to veranda at rear of house.

SIDE VIEW *(RIGHT)*
The sloping roof, the stilts that raise the house, the outside staircases, and the verandas are all typical features of a Guyanese house. The house was designed as a plaything, so the windows were left unglazed.

Lift-off roof painted with aluminum paint to suggest corrugated-iron finish.

Ruled lines on exterior walls represent planks.

Staircase made from plywood, with pine rail.

Canvas hammock slung under house.

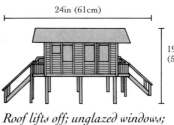

24in (61cm)

19½in (50cm)

Roof lifts off; unglazed windows; open doorways.

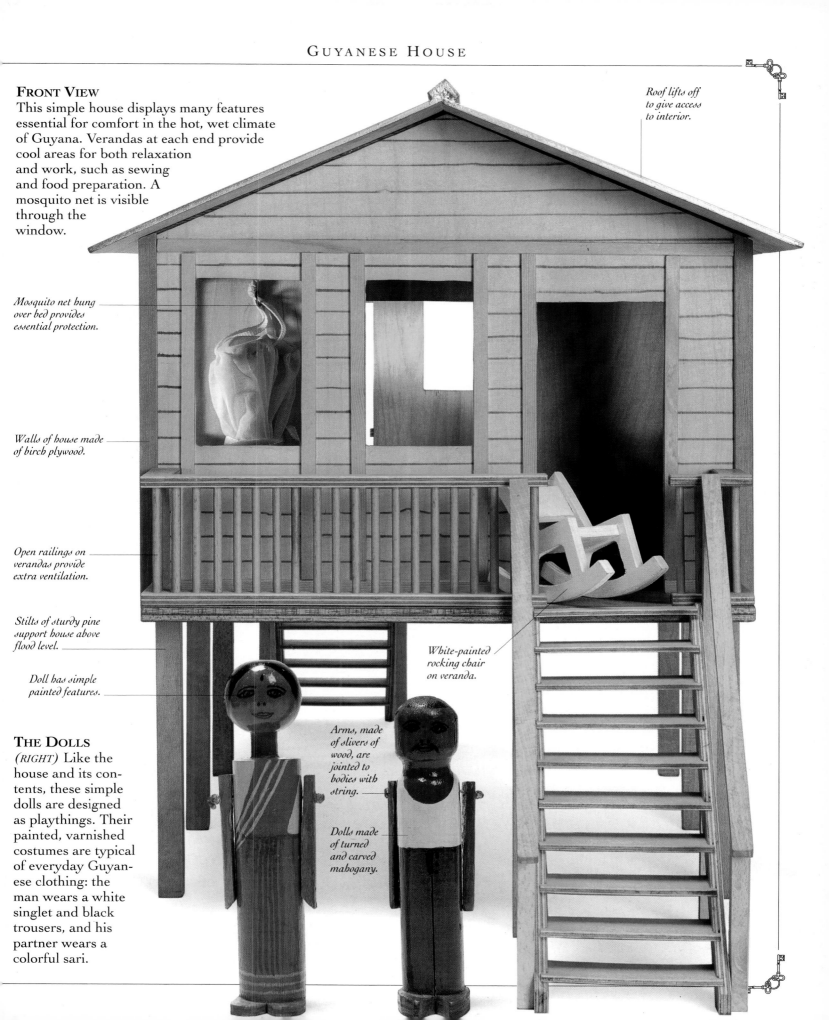

FRONT VIEW
This simple house displays many features essential for comfort in the hot, wet climate of Guyana. Verandas at each end provide cool areas for both relaxation and work, such as sewing and food preparation. A mosquito net is visible through the window.

Roof lifts off to give access to interior.

Mosquito net hung over bed provides essential protection.

Walls of house made of birch plywood.

Open railings on verandas provide extra ventilation.

Stilts of sturdy pine support house above flood level.

Doll has simple painted features.

White-painted rocking chair on veranda.

THE DOLLS
(RIGHT) Like the house and its contents, these simple dolls are designed as playthings. Their painted, varnished costumes are typical of everyday Guyanese clothing: the man wears a white singlet and black trousers, and his partner wears a colorful sari.

Arms, made of slivers of wood, are jointed to bodies with string.

Dolls made of turned and carved mahogany.

CONTAINER HOUSES

Miniature houses with a practical purpose

FOR CENTURIES, houses have provided inspiration for the design of containers. House-shaped sewing boxes, made from ivory or bone, were popular in Britain in the nineteenth century (Chinese straw-work boxes with removable roofs/lids are a modern version). Fragrant incense-burners and ceramic night-light holders, in the guise of cottages, houses, and even of castles, were popular with the Victorians, while music boxes housed in miniature Swiss chalets are long-standing favorites. House-shaped charity collection boxes are practical adaptations, while other dual-purpose containers include lunch boxes and handbags for children. Most container houses, however, are colorfully printed tins and cardboard boxes, often filled with edible goods or items such as china or writing paper.

STRAW-WORK BOX *(BELOW)*
This well-constructed model represents the US Capitol in Washington, D.C. Chinese straw-work boxes, which are rapidly becoming collectors' items, are usually small and colorful oriental-style houses.

Slit for coins to be dropped into house.

Painted papier-mâché charity box.

Printed tin with different design on each side.

Glued-on printed paper window.

HOUSE TIN *(ABOVE)*
Decorative house-shaped tins range from small, flat pill-boxes to tall house shapes, of the type shown above. They are usually made with removable or hinged lids, representing the roofs of the buildings.

SWISS MUSIC BOX *(BELOW)* Music boxes have always been one of Switzerland's most popular souvenirs. This carved and painted wooden example dates from the 1930s.

Top section lifts off to reveal padded space in base.

COLLECTION BOX *(ABOVE)*
Miniature houses make ideal collection boxes for charity. Dr. Barnardo's Homes (now known as Barnardo's) used boxes like this one in the UK until 1971.

Hinged roof allows access to musical mechanism.

Straw pillars adorn facade.

Base raised on four legs.

Winding key under base.

THE PRACTICALITIES

If the dolls' houses in this book have inspired you to start your own collection, this practical section will give you firsthand advice on where to start and what to look for, as well as tips on identifying miniatures. The hints on conservation and restoration will be useful if you already own a dolls' house or plan to acquire an old one.

• GOTTSCHALK HOUSE •
This c.1900–1910 German example illustrates a number of problems likely to be found in old dolls' houses.

COLLECTING DOLLS' HOUSES

DOLLS' HOUSE HUNTING is now easier, though more costly, than it was a few decades ago. It is no longer thought odd for adults to buy miniature houses for themselves as well as for children: in Europe and in the United States, collectors' clubs and magazines flourish and "for sale" advertisements are commonplace. If you are a prospective buyer, you can look for a house at auctions, specialty shops, or at toy and dolls' house fairs; and if you want a really special house, you can commission a craftsman to design and build one to your individual requirements.

— PRELIMINARY RESEARCH —

Whatever type of house you decide on, it is usually helpful to do some research first. If you are particularly interested in antique dolls' houses, libraries and bookstores now stock a splendid selection of well-illustrated books, many of which have been written by experts on the subject.

Museums, of course, are immensely useful for research and provide an opportunity to view for yourself some of the houses you may already have

TEACHING TOYS
(RIGHT) Dolls' houses have always been popular gifts for little girls. Mothers, regarding them as educational toys, fondly hoped the child would learn the principles of good housekeeping as she played.

seen illustrated in books; they may also enable you to see the size of a particular dolls' house, which can be an important consideration if space is limited.

Unless you have already found your "dream house" in a store, an auction house is probably the next place to visit. Most have items on display for a day or so before sales (dates are advertised in newspapers and magazines), and catalogs are available. But do inspect everything carefully; however charming a dolls' house may be, if it is affected by dry rot or woodworm it will need

AUCTION HOUSE *(LEFT) In front of the rostrum at Christie's auction house in London, Olivia Bristol, Christie's doll and dolls' house expert, views two items from a forthcoming sale. Auction house staff will give expert advice and valuations on request.*

ANNUAL FAIR *(RIGHT) Dolls' house and miniature fairs are held regularly in many countries. The booth of dolls' house maker Peter Mattinson at the London Dolls' House Festival, an annual event, is shown here.*

MASTER MINIATURIST
(LEFT) Leading miniaturist John Hodgson creates exquisite furniture as well as miniature buildings to house them. Some, including the Georgian House, are on display at Hever Castle, Kent, England (see pp.48–51).

DOLLS' HOUSE MUSEUM
(RIGHT) Privately owned museums are especially useful when the owner's knowledge is reflected in carefully selected exhibitions. Flora Gill Jacobs displays a fascinating collection of dolls' houses and rooms at her museum in Washington, D.C.

careful thought before purchase – and thoughtful care afterward. Dolls' house fairs are also worth visiting; most have booths selling houses, furnishings, and accessories, both old and new. The bigger fairs attract sellers from home and abroad, so the range of goods for sale is often extensive.

Another advantage of attending a fair is the opportunity it provides to talk to dolls' house makers. Many of these craftsmen and women rent booths to display their houses, and they are always willing to discuss building plans with prospective customers. They also supply the specialty dolls' house shops that, although virtually unknown 25 years ago, now offer an indispensable service to enthusiasts and collectors.

— KITS AND CUSTOMIZED HOUSES —

Specialty stores also supply the books and kits you need if you decide to make your own dolls' house; the shop's owner will be happy to offer advice or to recommend professional dolls' house makers who design and build on commission.

The high cost of antique and custom-made dolls' houses has encouraged many people to buy dolls' houses that were originally designed as children's playthings and to adapt them to their own requirements. This is one way of having an exclusive dolls' house although, obviously, it will not really compete with the professionally made ones in the recognized 1:12 collector's scale. Custom-made houses will have more realistically proportioned rooms and staircases, for example,

and may reflect a particular house style, or even reproduce one particular building in miniature.

Another option, if funds are limited, is to make a house from a standard kit, and then to embellish the basic building with your own individual touches. For example, you can produce authentic miniature replicas of photographs from a family album by reducing the full-scale originals to the required size on a photocopying machine. The creative possibilities are endless – and are all part of the fascination for the dolls' house enthusiast.

LONDON DOLLS' HOUSE SHOP *(ABOVE)*
Shops specializing in dolls' houses and miniatures are invaluable to collectors trying to track down individual items. Michal Morse has catered to both collectors and children since opening Britain's first specialty shop, The Dolls' House, in London in 1971.

DOCUMENTING MINIATURES

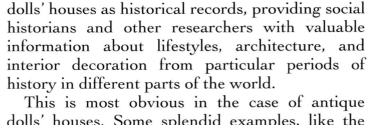

IN ADDITION TO the sheer pleasure that they find in miniatures and dolls' houses, collectors and enthusiasts have another, more academic interest in the subject. One aspect of this arises from the function of miniatures and

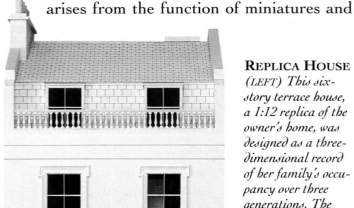

REPLICA HOUSE *(LEFT) This six-story terrace house, a 1:12 replica of the owner's home, was designed as a three-dimensional record of her family's occupancy over three generations. The front and back walls open, as do sections in one side, so that the rooms, the staircase with its cast-metal balusters, and the stained-glass windows (all exact replicas) can be seen more easily.*

dolls' houses as historical records, providing social historians and other researchers with valuable information about lifestyles, architecture, and interior decoration from particular periods of history in different parts of the world.

This is most obvious in the case of antique dolls' houses. Some splendid examples, like the baby house at Nostell Priory, do resemble the mansions in which they are still displayed; a few, such as the *c.*1740 King's Lynn baby house, are exact replicas of their original owners' homes.

— ORIGINAL RECORDS —

It sometimes happens, though sadly all too seldom, that the provenance of a dolls' house has been recorded and kept with it: Uppark's baby house is one very well-known English example. In Holland, Sara Ploos van Amstel kept meticulously detailed notebooks, which relate to the making and furnishing of her two famous cabinet houses *(see pp.34–37)*, and these are the most satisfying references that any researcher could desire.

Collectors today are aware that even modern, twentieth-century dolls' houses will become valuable research material for historians in the future, especially if both the interiors and facades of the houses are authentic replicas. With this in mind, some set out to reconstruct, in miniature, their own homes and day-to-day lives, or other examples from contemporary society. Such a project

CALLCOTT LABEL (*RIGHT*)
This label, which almost covers the base of a small papier-mâché house, made in 1914 (see pp.72–73), identifies the latter as a commercially made British product.

AVERY CHAIR (*LEFT/ABOVE*)
The English needle manufacturer W. Avery & Son of Redditch, Worcestershire, started making metal needlecases shaped like pieces of furniture in the 1860s. Its clearly stamped pieces are a joy to researchers.

could prove expensive if the fixtures and furniture as well as the house are made to order. It is possible to chronicle family or local history on a more modest scale, however, by commissioning, or even making, a cardboard or molded plaster model with accurately painted details. Even such simplified records merit labels of some kind; it is important, not only to the creators of modern miniature replicas, but to future researchers also, that the maker's name and the date and address of the full-scale house be documented in or on the miniature version. For a house to be regarded as an authentic historical record, this is essential.

— THE IMPORTANCE OF LABELS —

This brings us to another area of great interest to collectors: that of identifying and authenticating dolls' houses, dolls, and dolls' house furniture, and the difficulty of doing so without the aid of labels or records. Certainly, collectors and researchers bless those manufacturers whose names can be

BLISS FURNITURE (*LEFT*)
Though best known for its dolls' houses, the American firm Bliss of Pawtucket also made sets of furniture. One c.1901 Bliss line had pieces decorated with letters of the alphabet. There were several sets, mainly parlor and bedroom furniture, with different designs and colors. Although each piece had letters, usually printed in brown or red, the surrounding decoration varied from a simple scroll to a complicated design incorporating figures of children.

SCHOENHUT LABEL
(*RIGHT*) *Although it is fairly easy to recognize a Schoenhut dolls' house, a label is always a bonus.*

BLISS LABEL (*RIGHT*)
The name on many Bliss houses is incorporated into the chromo-lithographed design of the facade, as on the example shown here (see pp.90–91).

found on their products. Whether they use glued-on labels or employ designs with the name incorporated into a pattern, firms such as Bliss and Schoenhut deserve praise and gratitude.

Most infuriating and regrettable are the omissions of those artist-craftsmen and other small firms whose products were sold without any identifying marks. One craftswoman, Florence Callcott, has added greatly to the interest of her creations with her illustrated label, which is almost as big as the base of her little house (*see above*). On the other hand, the 1930s handcrafted Westacre Village "lacquered" dolls' house furniture and the tin pieces produced by a well-established firm, Evans & Cartwright, in the early nineteenth century have only recently been identified after researchers' painstaking efforts.

In the absence of trademarks, collectors have to rely on their knowledge and experience when attempting to identify or authenticate a piece – knowledge gathered from extensive reading, visits to museums, talking to other collectors, and the ongoing research that provides so much interest for those involved in the world of miniatures.

RESTORATION AND CONSERVATION

IT IS SOMETIMES difficult to decide how, or even if, an antique dolls' house should be restored. Pending expert advice, a good rule is "when in doubt, do nothing." Often, more damage is done by restoration than by the ravages of time, reducing both the historical interest and the monetary value of the house in question.

However, if an antique dolls' house has been painted over, papered with modern wallpapers, or given synthetic curtains, these should be removed and, if possible, old papers and fabrics used instead. You can sometimes find old worn shawls, clothing, and odd ends of wallpapers in junk shops or at rummage sales; old workbaskets may contain scraps of antique fabric, braid, or lace that may also prove useful.

Woodworm and dry rot must be treated immediately. Such problems, along with any damage to woodwork, or corroded or rusted metalwork, require expert advice, and possibly professional treatment, before any restoration work is attempted.

Whether to install electric lighting is a personal choice, but in general it is not advisable if the dolls' house was made before such lighting would have been used in a similar, full-scale house.

Careful conservation, including keeping dolls' houses away from direct heat, light, or damp, and regular housekeeping, will ensure well-being and minimize any future restoration problem.

MUSEUM CONSERVATOR
(ABOVE) Ella Hendricks, conservator at the Frans Halsmuseum in Haarlem, Holland, is shown at work on one of the outer doors of Sara Ploos van Amstel's cabinet house (see pp.34–37).

Peeling wallpaper.

Graffiti on wallpaper can be hidden by furniture if not removable.

Replacement glass required for window.

Vertical break in facade needs repair.

Modern wrapping paper used to paper this room.

Damage to "stonework" can be filled in.

Slight water stain on brick-effect base paper.

BLISS HOUSE WINDOW

(RIGHT) The painted window on the ground floor of this otherwise delightful small Bliss house is neither the original nor a correct replica. Someone has reproduced the design of the painted upper windows, but research would have shown that this window was originally glazed. Glass should replace the painted window to restore the house to its original appearance.

Roof has been painted over.

EXTERIOR PROBLEMS

UNRESTORED ORIGINAL
(ABOVE) Opinions vary on how much active repairing is acceptable. In this case the owner chose to retain the original, damaged paintwork rather than to paint over the missing section.

MISSING DOOR *(ABOVE) In this example, the missing door severely affects the look of the dolls' house, and it would be reasonable to replace it with a replica copied from the door on an identical model.*

DAMAGED DOLLS' HOUSE

(LEFT) Conservation alone is not enough for this Gottschalk house, but, with replica replacement doors and windows, repairs on the facade, and the removal of modern wallpapers and newer painting on the roof, door, and facade interior, it may again become a desirable residence.

Mended facade requires new hinges, put in original positions.

Door painted over.

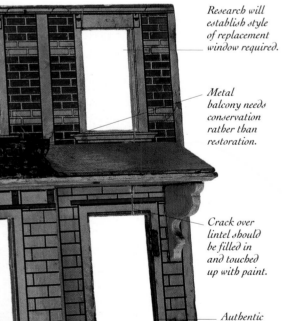

Research will establish style of replacement window required.

Metal balcony needs conservation rather than restoration.

Crack over lintel should be filled in and touched up with paint.

Authentic replacement for missing door required.

Wrinkled floor paper; not original.

LOST FACADE DETAIL
(ABOVE) The missing quoining on the corner will not hasten the deterioration of this dolls' house; whether it should be replaced is, therefore, a matter of personal opinion about conservation.

DAMAGED ROOF *(ABOVE) The deterioration on the roof of this Schoenhut bungalow may become worse and, if the corner is bumped, the damage could be serious. Restoration now appears to be the sensible option.*

INTERIOR PROBLEMS

TORN WALLPAPER *(ABOVE) It is unlikely that you will find a matching piece to replace torn or missing wallpaper, and replicas are usually unconvincing. Many collectors hide such a loss with a picture or a piece of furniture.*

REPLACEMENT CURTAINS
(ABOVE) Pieces from an old paisley shawl, or scraps of old fabrics, will provide excellent curtains for an antique dolls' house. Use old wooden or bone knitting needles for curtain rods.

ADDRESSES

CANADA

DAISY DOLLHOUSE
P.O. Box 92
Flatbush, Alta, TOG OZO

THE DOLL ATTIC & CO.
62 Brock Street
Kingston, Ont., K7L 1R9

THE LITTLE DOLLHOUSE CO.
617 Mt. Pleasant Road
Toronto, Ont., M4S 2M5

ROSS' TREASURE HOUSE LTD
823 1st Street West
North Vancouver
B.C. V7P 1A4

DENMARK

LEGOLAND PARK
Nordmarksvej 9
DK-7190 Billund

FRANCE

MUSEE DES ARTS DECORATIFS
Départment Jouets
Palais du Louvre
107 rue de Rivoli
75001 Paris

MUSEE HISTORIC DU JOUET
2 Enclos de L'Arbayr
78300 Poissy

GERMANY

BAYERN STADTMUSEUM
Postfach 80331
München

GERMANISCHES NATIONALMUSEUM
Kornmarkt 1
8500 Nürnberg

SPIELZEUGMUSEUM
Karlstrasse 13
8500 Nürnberg

HOLLAND

CENTRAAL MUSEUM
Agnietenstraat 1
NL 3500, GC Utrecht

FRANS HALSMUSEUM
P.O. Box 3365
2001 DJ Haarlem

GEMEENTEMUSEUM
Stadhouderslaan 41
25178V The Hague

RIJKSMUSEUM
P.O. Box 74888
1070 DN Amsterdam

SWEDEN

NORDISKA MUSEET
Djugårdsvägen 6–16
115 93 Stockholm

SWITZERLAND

HAUS ZUM KIRSCHGARTEN
Elisabethenstrasse 27
CH-4051 Basel

UNITED KINGDOM

BETHNAL GREEN MUSEUM OF CHILDHOOD
Cambridge Heath Road
London E2 9PA

DOLLS' HOUSE MUSEUM
23 High Street
Arundel
W. Sussex BN18 9AD

MUSEUM OF CHILDHOOD
42 High Street
Edinburgh EH1 1TG

MUSEUM OF CHILDHOOD
117 Main Street
Haworth
Keighley
Yorkshire BD22 8DU

MUSEUM OF CHILDHOOD
Church Street
Ribchester
Lancashire PR3 3YE

MUSEUM OF CHILDHOOD
Sudbury Hall
Sudbury
Derbyshire DE6 5HT

POLLOCK'S TOY MUSEUM
1 Scala Street
London W1P 1LT

PRESTON HALL MUSEUM
Yarm Road
Stockton-on-Tees
Cleveland TS18 3RH

TOY & TEDDY MUSEUM
373 Clifton Drive North
Lytham St Anne's
Lancashire FY8 2PA

VIVIEN GREENE COLLECTION
The Rotunda
Grove House
Iffley Turn
Oxford, OX4 4DU
(Private collection; viewing by prior arrangement only; no children under 16)

WARWICK DOLLS' MUSEUM
Oken House
Warwick
Warwickshire CV34 4BP

A WORLD IN MINIATURE
North Pier, Oban
Argyll PA34 5QD

WORTHING MUSEUM
Chapel Road
Worthing
W. Sussex BN11 1HP

USA

ANGEL'S ATTIC
516 Colorado Avenue
Santa Monica, Calif.
90401–2408

MARGARET WOODBURY STRONG MUSEUM
1 Manhattan Square
Rochester, N.Y. 14607

MUSEUM OF THE CITY OF NEW YORK
1220 Fifth Avenue
New York, N.Y. 10029

MUSEUM OF SCIENCE AND INDUSTRY
5700 Lakeshore Drive
Chicago, Ill. 60637

SMITHSONIAN INSTITUTION
Museum of American History
Washington, D.C. 20560

TOY & MINIATURE MUSEUM
5235 Oak Street
Kansas City, Mo. 64112

WASHINGTON DOLLS' HOUSE & TOY MUSEUM
5236 44th Street N.W.
Washington, D.C. 20015

DRAPERY SHOP *(LEFT)*
Though basically just a cardboard box, whose hinged lid folds forward to form the tiled-effect floor, this type of shop was a popular plaything during the 1930s. Both the dolls – a shop assistant and customer inspecting a bolt of material – are cheap, German, pegged-wooden dolls, c.1920s, wearing original clothes.

GLOSSARY

ALCOVE Vaulted recess in wall.
ARCHITRAVE Molding around doorway or window; beam resting on upper part of pillar.
BABY HOUSE English term for miniature house in seventeenth and eighteenth centuries.
BALUSTER Pillar or post supporting handrail.
BALUSTRADE Railing supported by row of balusters.
BAROUCHE Four-wheeled horse-drawn carriage.
BAY Projecting window.
BEVEL Angle, other than right angle, between two surfaces.
BIEDERMEIER Style of conventional furniture popular in Germany, 1810–45.
BISQUE Unglazed porcelain.
CABINET HOUSE Cabinet (often Dutch) adapted as miniature house, containing collection of objets d'art.
CABRIOLE LEG Type of leg on furniture with upper convex curve tapering to lower concave curve.

CASEMENT WINDOW Vertically hinged window.
CHAFING DISH Dish with heating device underneath for keeping food warm at the table.
CHROMOLITHOGRAPHY Printing technique for producing colored prints.
CLAVICHORD Keyboard instrument with thin wire strings.
COMPTOIR Room used as office.
CORBEL Stone or timber bracket providing support.
CORNICE Molding along top of building, or just below ceiling.
CREEL Wickerwork basket.
CUPBOARD HOUSE Cupboard converted to contain miniature, furnished rooms.
DADO Lower part of wall, decorated separately.
DECOUPAGE Surface decorated with shapes or illustrations cut from paper.
DORMER Vertical window, set in sloping roof.
EAVES Area of roof projecting beyond wall.

ENTABLATURE Architrave, frieze, and cornice resting on columns.
ENTRESOL Low story between first and second floors.
ESCUTCHEON Metal plate surrounding keyhole.
FAIENCE Decorated porcelain or earthenware.
FASCIA Flat, vertical surface above store window.
FANLIGHT Semicircular window positioned above door, often with radiating mullions.
FICHU Woman's scarf or shawl of light material, popular in eighteenth century.
FINIAL Decorative addition to top of post or gable.
FLAGSTONES Large stone slabs used for paving.
FONTANGE Towering headdress of ribbon and lace, popular in England in seventeenth century.
FRETWORK Decorative wood carving or openwork.
FRIEZE Horizontal decoration at top of wall.
GABLE Triangular section of wall at end of ridged roof.
GEORGIAN Period in British history c.1714–1830; style of architecture and furniture popular in eighteenth century.
HALF-TESTER BED Bed with canopy over head end.
JABOT Ruffle or frill worn at neck of garment.
JARDINIERE Ornamental pot or stand for plants.
KEYSTONE Central stone of arch.
LAPPETS Small flaps of lace hanging from headdress.
LYING-IN ROOM Room for confinement in childbirth.

BLUE-ROOF HOUSE

(LEFT) Although it looks similar to many lithographed, Bliss-type American houses, this model is German, made c.1900. It is probably from the line of "blue-roof" dolls' houses made after the mid-nineteenth century in Moritz Gottschalk's works in Marienberg, Germany.

OBJET D'ART Small object of artistic merit.
MANSARD ROOF Roof with two slopes on each side; the lower slopes are steeper.
MODILLION Ornamental bracket under cornice.
MULLIONS Wooden bars holding window panes in position.
NICHE Decorative recess in wall.
ORMOLU Gold-colored alloy.
PALLADIAN Style of architecture characterized by symmetry and harmonious proportions.
PEDIMENT Triangular section above door or window.
PEWTER Alloy containing tin, lead, and sometimes other metals.
PICTURE RAIL Wood or metal rail from which pictures are hung.
PROVENANCE Proof of place of origin of work of art.
QUOINS Cornerstones.
RISER Flat, vertical section of step or stair.
ROCOCO Elaborate style of architecture and decoration.
SASH WINDOW Window that slides up and down in grooves.
SCONCE Wall bracket holding candles and lights.
SKIRTING BOARD Wooden section along bottom of wall.
SPLAT Central part of chair back.
STUART Relating to period of British architecture c.1603–49.
TERRA-COTTA Brownish red, unglazed earthenware.
TETE-A-TETE S-shaped sofa for two people, allowing them to sit almost face to face.
TORCHERE Tall narrow stand holding candelabrum.
TREAD Flat, horizontal section of step or stair.
TROMPE L'OEIL Painting that gives illusion of reality.
TRUG Long, shallow basket for flowers, fruit, or vegetables.
TYMPANUM Triangular space between arch and lintel of doorway, or pediment's cornices.
VICTORIAN Relating to period of British history 1837–1901.
VIRGINAL Small tabletop version of harpsichord.
WAINSCOT Lower interior wall section, often paneled in wood.

INDEX

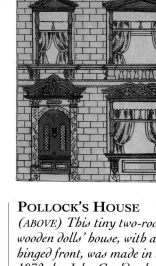

POLLOCK'S HOUSE

(*ABOVE*) *This tiny two-room wooden dolls' house, with a hinged front, was made in the 1970s by John Gould, who used one of Mr Pollock's nineteenth-century hand-colored prints – depicting a brick wall with door and windows – as a facade.*

WOODEN DOLLS' HOUSE FURNITURE (*LEFT*)

These simple little pieces were selected to furnish a c.1917 Schoenhut bungalow. Metal and-irons hold the logs in a wooden fireplace with red brick-effect background; the small lamp is a modern, plastic replica.

LIGHT FIXTURE (*ABOVE*)
Known as a "gasolier," this gilded lead light fixture, with milk-glass globes, is from a c.1880 French parlor. When electricity became popular, manufacturers adapted such fixtures by hanging them upside down and using down-pointing bulbs and shades instead of globes.

***c.*1900 LINEN CUPBOARD** (*LEFT*)
Well stocked with household linen, bolts of cotton, sheets, and even mattress stuffing, this decorative, painted wooden cupboard is a miniature version of the traditional linen cupboard that formed an important part of the dowries of southern German and Austrian brides.

AMERICAN DOLLS' HOUSE
*(RIGHT) The earliest known
American dolls' house, this
simple structure (dated 1744)
has two rooms back and front
with built-in fireplaces and
painted windows on the sides.*

ACKNOWLEDGMENTS

AUTHOR'S ACKNOWLEDGMENTS

Many people have shared their knowledge and opened their dolls'
houses to be photographed for this book. My most grateful thanks
go particularly to Flora Gill Jacobs who, with her husband Ephraim,
so graciously and helpfully made our time in their home and at the
Washington Dolls' House & Toy Museum a very special episode.

Private collectors in England, too, unfailingly made their dolls'
houses – and often their own homes – available to us; my special
thanks go to Peggy and Dick Allen, Olivia Bristol, Moira Garland,
Janet Gent, Michal Morse, and Suzie Vincent.

We were privileged also to be able to photograph dolls' houses in
stately homes, museums, a shop, and an auction house; for their
invaluable cooperation, my most appreciative thanks go to: Lord and
Lady St. Oswald and the staff at Nostell Priory; Roger Whitworth at
the National Trust; John Guthrie and Claire Proùt at Hever Castle;
John Hodgson; Ann Jones and the staff at the Museum of Farnham;
Dr. Michael Eissenhauer, Dr. Hermann Maué, and Dr. Ulrike
Heinrichs at the Germanisches Nationalmuseum, Nuremberg; Ella
Hendricks and Helen Joustra at Frans Halsmuseum, Haarlem;
Charlie Koens and Jurjen Creman at Centraal Museum, Haarlem;
Juliet Wiggins at Playmobil (UK) Ltd; Mr. and Mrs. Pickering of
the International Doll and Toy Collection; Michal Morse of The
Dolls' House; and Olivia Bristol and Christine Jeffery at Christie's,
South Kensington.

My thanks go to everyone at Dorling Kindersley who helped
with the book – an extra thank you to Andrea Fair for deciphering
my handwriting – with my warmest thanks to the Indomitable Trio,
editor Irene Lyford, art editor Kevin Ryan, and photographer
Matthew Ward, without whom the book could not have been produced and whose inspiration was matched only by their patience.

PUBLISHER'S ACKNOWLEDGMENTS

Dorling Kindersley would like to thank: Mr. and Mrs. Jacobs and the
staff of the Washington Dolls' House & Toy Museum, Washington,
D.C., for their very generous help and hospitality; Olivia Bristol for
her unstinting help, expertise, and hospitality; staff at Nostell Priory,
Wakefield; Germanisches Nationalmuseum, Nuremberg; Centraal
Museum, Utrecht; and Frans Halsmuseum, Haarlem for invaluable
access to collections, help, and advice; Andrea Fair for unfailing
support, and for magically transforming handwritten copy into
on-screen text; Charlotte Davies and Gillian
Roberts for greatly appreciated editorial
assistance; Michael Allaby for compiling the
index; Julia Pashley for picture research;
Murdo Culver for design assistance; and
David Lyford for making
the room set on page 11.
In particular they would
like to thank Matthew
Ward and his assistant
Rachel Leach for their
unflagging patience and
good humor in often
difficult conditions.

COMMISSIONED ARTWORKS

We thank **Stephen Dew** for the house scale diagrams and other
linework, and **Janos Marffy** for airbrush shadows.

PICTURE CREDITS

*In the following acknowledgments, abbreviations with page numbers indicate
position on page: t=top; b=bottom; c=center; l=left; r=right*

Bridgeman Art Library/Phillips 9tl; Christie's Fine Art Auctioneers
52bl, 132bl; Civico Museo Industriale Davia Bargelliri di Bologna
16b; Mary Evans Picture Library 6t, 132tr; Dave King Photo Library
143b; Peter Mattinson 132br; Nick Nicholson 7t, 7b, 14b, 15tl, 15tr,
15bl; Punch (1900) 140; The Royal Collection © Her Majesty Queen
Elizabeth II 16t.

DOLLS' HOUSE COLLECTIONS/OWNERS/MANUFACTURERS

Centraal Museum, Utrecht 8, 24–5, 26–7, 28–9; Christie's (South
Kensington) Ltd. 62–3, 82–3, 84–5, 135tl, 137bc, 139; Paul Cumbie 17;
The Dolls' House, Covent Garden 133br; *The Dolls' House Carousel* ©
Bellew Publishing, Maggie Bateson & Herman Lelie, published in UK
by Simon & Schuster 112tl; Dover Books: Sears, Roebuck & Co.
Catalogs 75t, The New Pretty Village 87tl, 87tr; Faith Eaton
Collection 3t, 4, 9tr, 11tr, 12bl, 12br, 13, 68–9, 76–7, 9, 72br, 73t, 94–5,
96–7, 98–9, 100–1, 102–3, 104–5, 110, 111b, 112tr, 112b, 113, 114–15,
116–17, 120–1, 122–3, 128–9, 130tr, 130br, 135tr, 137tc, 137tr, 137cl,
137br, 138, 141t, 142b; Museum of Farnham (long-term loan) 10t;
Frans Halsmuseum, Haarlem 11tl, 34–5, 36–7, 136bl; Courtesy Moira
Garland 54t, 119t; Janet Gent 137tl; Germanisches Nationalmuseum,
Nuremberg 2, 18–19, 20–1, 22–3, 30–1, 32–3; Hever Castle Limited
11b, 48–9, 50–1, 133tl; Irene Lyford 130c; Mattel UK Ltd. 113; Michal
Morse Collection 11tr (contents); 72bl, 80–1; National Trust/St
Oswald Collection: gatefold section; The Pickering Collection, Ethnic
Doll & Toy Museum, England 53t, 124–5, 126–7; Playmobil (UK) Ltd
106–7, 108–9; Private Collections 1, 3b, 12t, 38–9, 40–1, 52br, 55b,
64–5, 74b, 131, 134br, 134tl, 136–7; Kevin Ryan 130bl; S.R. Vincent
53b, 75b, 86, 87bl, 87br, 111t, 141b; Washington Dolls' House & Toy
Museum 5, 6b, 10b, 42–3, 44–5, 46–7, 54b, 55t, 56–7, 58–9, 60–1, 66–7,
70–1, 73b, 74t, 88–9, 90–1, 92–3, 118, 119b, 133tr, 135cr, 135br, 137cr,
137c, 142–3t, 144.

Every effort has been made
to acknowledge owners and
copyright holders. Dorling
Kindersley apologizes for
any omissions.

HOUSE AND GARDEN

*When the ingenious
hinged garden folds
up, its base forms the
fourth wall of this
decorative twentieth-
century German "red-
roof" dolls' house with
balconies, porch, and
an ornamental gabled
attic roof.*